Yamamba

Yamamba

In Search of the Japanese Mountain Witch

Edited by
Rebecca Copeland and Linda C. Ehrlich

Stone Bridge Press • *Berkeley, California*

Published by
Stone Bridge Press
P. O. Box 8208, Berkeley, CA 94707
TEL 510-524-8732 • sbp@stonebridge.com • www.stonebridge.com

Cover design by Linda Ronan.

Illustrations for cover, "Yamamba's Mountains," and "Yamamba's Laughter and Other Poems" by Maria Alilovic, with dancing figure based on the Noh play *Yamamba*.

Frontispiece and back-cover calligraphy "Yamamba" by Ohmori Kayo.

"The Smile of a Mountain Witch," translated by Noriko Mizuta Lippit, assisted by Mariko Ochi, with the permission of the author. From *Japanese Women Writers: Twentieth-Century Short Fiction* by Kyoko Iriye Selden and Noriko Mizuta Lippit. Reproduced by permission of Taylor and Francis Group, LLC, a division of informa plc. ©1991.

Photograph on page 132 courtesy of Kinosaki International Arts Center (Toyooka City), Izushi Eirakukan, 2019.

Printed in the United States of America.

10 9 8 7 6 5 4 3 2 1   2025 2024 2023 2022 2021

p-ISBN 978-1-61172-066-2
e-ISBN 978-1-61172-948-1

Contents

Beyond Place, Before Time— Why We Seek the Yamamba

Rebecca Copeland and Linda C. Ehrlich

> mountain witch
> mountain crone
> mountain hag

Her name in Japanese and its romanization are just as varied:

> yamamba
> yamanba
> yamauba

The repetition of her name resembles a magic chant, a mantra, a curse. And like the natural stronghold that contains her—rocky ridges and soft glens—she is alluring, nurturing, dangerous, and vulnerable. What is it about the fusion of mountains with the solitary old woman that produces this phenomenon, this enigmatic figure? How is it that one so singular and unprotected can ignite such fear?

But not only fear. The mountain witch also beguiles. She tricks the innocent and unsuspecting in fairytales and legend to step inside her strange spaces where their fate becomes hers to determine. And she mesmerizes artists—playwrights, photographers, writers, and dancers—with her mercurial sway and outsider freedom. They are drawn to her for their creative vision, and she gladly answers, guiding their hands, their eyes, their hearts. Intellectuals, too, have sought the yamamba, hoping to find in her the source of ancient misogyny, the key to irrational superstition. She becomes the touchstone to inner passages of understanding, the container of unspoken desire, the measure of the unknown.

Yamamba: In Search of the Japanese Mountain Witch presents the eclectic responses engendered by the yamamba. From poetry and essays, to short stories and interviews, the works assembled here offer readers a sampling of the awe the yamamba inspires with her power. Our contributors range from university professors to professional choreographers. One feature these works share is an homage to the yamamba. They are our attempt to reflect her spirit creatively. While already many works have been written *about* the yamamba, as our list of recommended readings at the end of this book suggests, this is the first work in English to be written *for* the yamamba.

This unique collection represents creative imaginings and efforts from North America and Japan by those who have encountered the yamamba in their work. We open with a decidedly scholarly account of our muse by Noriko T. Reider, an expert on Japanese folklore, that sets the stage for all readers. And from there we proceed along mountain paths into dark caverns and sunny glades in search of the yamamba.

HOW WE MET THE YAMAMBA

Anthologies start with a glimmer of an idea and spark into a bright light when nurtured by like-minded people. Some anthologies take years to complete; others rapidly fall into place. *Yamamba: In Search of the Japanese Mountain Witch* fits into the latter category. But the idea behind this collection was one that ripened over two careers.

Co-editors Rebecca Copeland and Linda C. Ehrlich, both academic researchers and instructors, first met the yamamba in the powerful short story "The Smile of a Mountain Witch" by acclaimed woman writer Ōba Minako. Translated by Noriko Mizuta Lippit, then a professor of comparative literature at the University of Southern California, the story revealed the compelling way creative women can take charge of misogynistic tropes, invert them, and use them to tell new stories of female empowerment. This work became our starting point, leading us deeper into encounters with the yamamba, with ourselves, and eventually with each other.

Linda C. Ehrlich's long poem "Yamamba's Mountains" continues the style of writing and the tone of her prose poetry in *Cinematic Reveries* (Peter Lang, 2013). It also draws on her training in Asian Theatre from the University of Hawaii and her guest lectures for the Noh Training Project (Bloomsburg, PA/ Kyoto, Japan) and the Where Rivers Meet festival (held in San Antonio, TX). Thanks to the contributions of two fine visual artists and the brilliant work of Horse and Buggy Press's designer, she published the poem in a limited letterpress edition.

Simultaneously, Rebecca Copeland had been working on essays devoted to the yamamba, most notably "Mythical

Bad Girls: The Corpse, the Crone, and the Snake" (*Bad Girls of Japan*, eds. Miller and Bardsley, Palgrave MacMillan, 2005), which featured a creative preface in the imagined voice of the mountain witch. Copeland's essay captured the eye of dancer and choreographer Yokoshi Yasuko, who was herself working on a dance inspired by the fifteenth-century Japanese playwright Zeami's ode to the yamamba. Ehrlich sent Copeland a copy of her poem. Yokoshi invited her to attend her performance in Kyoto. The yamamba beckoned us all and we answered.

Ehrlich and Copeland called on others to join in their quest for the yamamba. She is everywhere. As Laura Miller beautifully illustrates, the yamamba crosses easily into a Latin American context. Rebecca Copeland finds the yamamba in the Appalachian Mountains. The yamamba reaches back to the medieval period in the informed testimony of professional Noh performers, the Uzawas (mother and daughter), interviewed by scholar of Japanese literature Ann Sherif.

The yamamba doesn't rest in the past. A contemporary yamamba bursts onto the stage in Yokoshi Yasuko's *shuffle-yamamba*. She inhabits Mizuta Noriko's dreams and emerges in her poetry, translated in this volume by Marianne Tarcov and Rebecca Copeland. She is everywhere that female voices have been repressed and where independent women have been castigated as witches. But she is also elusive. The yamamba is a figure of immensity. While not lacking in compassion, she transcends ordinary kindness. Other contributors to the anthology stress her fearful aspect or her connection to older myths. Scholar David Holloway sees the yamamba in the Aokigahara—the so-called "Suicide Forest" of eastern Japan—that has lately become a flashpoint of curiosity and controversy. The yamamba is generally viewed as feminine in nature, but surely all of us—men and women—have something of the yamamba in our *kokoro* (hearts and souls). We have drawn many incarnations of the yamamba in this volume; we await her next appearance with time.

Our collection stretches the parameters of scholarly writing and moves outside of the confines of the empirical essay. The yamamba would have it so. She leads us beyond the village, away from the order of academic knowledge. We wander into a landscape as full of possibilities as the yamamba's.

ACKNOWLEDGMENTS

Our thanks to Peter Goodman of Stone Bridge Press for his enthusiasm and expertise and for his willingness to support this unique window onto Japanese culture. Thanks also to the Uzawas (Hisa and Hikaru) and to Yokoshi Yasuko for graciously granting interviews for this anthology. Maria Alilovic's striking images contribute richly to this collection, as do the photographs provided by Kinosaki International Arts Center and the Uzawas. We are especially delighted to be able to include Ōba Minako's 1976 story "Yamauba no bishō" (The Smile of a Mountain Witch), translated by Noriko Mizuta Lippit with assistance from Mariko Ochi.

RC, LCE

REGARDING NAMES AND ROMANIZATION: In general, we list Japanese names in the traditional Japanese order, with surname first, unless the writer/speaker has an established identity in the English-language world, in which case we use surname last. The way Japanese is romanized has changed over time. Today, the standard romanization of *yamamba* is *yamanba*. But we have retained the older romanization throughout in keeping with the style used when we first encountered the Japanese mountain witch.

Locating the Yamamba

Noriko T. Reider *

Encounters with the mysterious and fearful often compel us to turn to the supernatural to help us make sense of the unknown. In Japan *yōkai* (weird or mysterious creatures) have frequently been called upon to explicate phenomena we cannot understand. A yamamba (yamauba or yamanba), often translated as a mountain witch or mountain crone, is one such being. To many contemporary Japanese, the word yamamba conjures up images of an unsightly old woman who lives in the mountains and devours humans. The witch in the Grimm Brothers' "Hansel and Gretel" and Baba Yaga of Russian folklore might be considered Western/Eurasian counterparts of the yamamba. One of the best known *yōkai* in Japan, the yamamba is commonly described as tall, with long hair, piercing eyes, and a large mouth that opens from ear to ear.

YAMAMBA STORIES

Whereas the yamamba appears in a variety of different guises

* This chapter is based on an excerpt from *Mountain Witches: Yamauba* (Logan: Utah State University Press, 2021). I am grateful to Utah State University Press for permission to use this selection here.

throughout Japanese history, let me introduce four representative texts that help to identify some of her attributes. We begin with *Yamamba*, an early fifteenth-century dramatic piece in the Noh performance tradition. The play introduces a female entertainer, known as Hyakuma Yamamba (hereafter Hyakuma), who is famous in the capital for performing the dance of the mythical yamamba. Hyakuma is on her way through the mountains when suddenly the sky turns as dark as night and the true Yamamba (the protagonist, with capital "Y" to avoid confusion) appears before her disguised as an old woman. Yamamba offers the dancer and her retinue lodging for the night but requests that Hyakuma sing her yamamba song. Yamamba thinks that Hyakuma should pay tribute to her, as the source of the entertainer's fame. Eventually, Yamamba reveals her true form to Hyakuma and offers her own yamamba dance, describing her mountain rounds, her association with nature, and the way she invisibly helps humans.

The second story is a folktale entitled "Kuwazu nyōbō" (The Wife Who Does Not Eat). The story opens with the mutterings of a man who longs for a wife who does not eat (and thus will not be expensive to keep). Almost immediately a beautiful young woman appears at his house and declares that she does not eat. The man takes her in, and she becomes his wife. But this seemingly ideal woman turns out to be a monster with an enormous mouth hidden at the back of her head. While she refrains from eating in the man's presence, as soon as he leaves she pulls her hair back from her hidden mouth and gorges herself. When the man eventually discovers the truth, the yamamba, now in her true form, throws him into a tub and carries him off toward the mountains. The man narrowly escapes, hides himself in a patch of mugwort and iris, and then throws the plants at her. Because these plants are highly toxic to the yamamba, she dies.

The third story is also a folktale. In "Komebuku Awabuku" (Komebuku and Awabuku), a mother gives a hole-riddled bag to her stepdaughter, Komebuku, and a good bag to her real daughter, Awabuku, and sends them to the mountains to collect chestnuts. The sun sets, and the two daughters lose their way. They find a house in the mountains that turns out to be a yamamba's house. In return for lodging the yamamba asks them to pick huge lice off her head. Komebuku complies, but Awabuku refuses. When they leave the house, the yamamba gives Komebuku a treasure box and Awabuku some roasted beans. The mother takes Awabuku to a theatrical play and has the stepdaughter stay at home to perform menial chores. But with the help of a traveling priest and a sparrow, Komebuku speedily finishes the tasks and goes to the play wearing beautiful clothes found in the treasure box the yamamba had given her. A young man who sees Komebuku at the play proposes marriage to her. The real daughter, wanting a husband of her own, sets out with her mother to find a suitor, but along the way they fall into a stream and turn into mud snails.[1]

The last yamamba reference derives from a legend, which tells of a yamamba giving birth to 7,800 children at one time. As it came time to deliver, the yamamba was (not surprisingly!) having difficulty. She asked a hunter who happened to be in the area at the time for water. Because he generously helped her deliver the 7,800 babies and name them, she rewarded him with an abundance of quarry.[2]

These four disparate vignettes reveal the complicated and

often contradictory attributes associated with the yamamba. She is associated with nature, as signified by her mountain topos (described below). Like nature she is erratic, changeable, at times malevolent, at times benevolent. One of her most constant attributes is her voracious appetite as suggested in the folktale "The Wife Who Does Not Eat." But, the yamamba is also known to be gentle and helpful, as seen in "Komebuku and Awabuku." A yamamba has the transformational power to manifest herself as an ugly crone or a young beauty. She can even manifest as objects or as nothing at all. Invisible yamamba also exist.

Some yamamba may desire to eat children, while others are depicted as bearing children. Occasionally, they are mothers to divine children. Perhaps the most famous example is that of Kintarō's mother. Kintarō, a boy with superhuman strength, is a popular character in folklore, Kabuki and puppet plays, and children's books and songs, and even is the namesake of candies called Kintarō amé. The yamamba's motherly aspects became well known during the early modern period (1600–1868) through legends, folktales, literary works, woodblock prints, and performing arts.

A yamamba is often associated with spinning and weaving. Interestingly, in many versions of "The Wife Who Does Not Eat," the real identity of the protagonist-wife is a spider, a creature known for spinning. The yamamba in some tales can foretell the future and read people's minds as seen in the folktale "Yamamba and the Cooper" and more recently in Ōba Minako's modern short story "The Smile of a Mountain Witch" (reprinted in this volume).

APPEARANCE OF THE TERM *YAMAMBA*

The first appearance of the term *yamamba* in literary materials occurred in the Muromachi period (1336–1573).[3] Prior to that, the enigmatic witch-like female one encountered in the mountains was often described as an *oni* (fierce demon, ogre, monster) or evil *oni*-woman. Between 1280 to 1450 the population in Japan expanded from around six million to about ten million, a 67 percent increase.[4] Historian Wayne Farris notes, "with the massive expansion of the old capital's population and religious and government building during Yoshimitsu's era [shogun 1358–1408], it is not surprising to find merchants going farther and farther afield to locate adequate supplies."[5] As more people went into the hitherto relatively unknown mountainous areas to cut trees or hunt, to travel through to a newly created marketplace, to transport goods, to travel for religious purposes, or simply to live, they probably would encounter various strange creatures and may have wondered what they were.

I suppose the term or signifier *yamamba* came into being because such women in the mountains, true or imagined, became more visible and noticeable to villagers and travelers. These mountain women could not be identified simply as *oni*—because they were also helpful at times or demonstrated positive characteristics. And so, the new term *yamamba* was perhaps devised to separate these mysterious mountain women from *oni*.

YAMAMBA'S TOPOS, MOUNTAINS

As Mizuta Noriko, a scholar of comparative literature, poet, and contributor to this volume, emphasizes, "Yamamba's identity is the topos of mountains."[6] Mountains are considered to be sacred places in many cultures, and this is true in Japan as well. Miyake Hitoshi, a scholar of religious studies, cites several reasons for this, and two of them are especially pertinent to our purposes here; one is that "mountains are viewed as the dwelling place of spirits of the dead and ancestor spirits. Tombs are built on mountains," and the other is that "mountains are regarded as a liminal space between this world and the otherworld. The mountain is an avenue to heaven; a mountain cave is an entrance to the otherworld."[7]

Poet and critic Baba Akiko emphasizes the importance of the way these tales are "grounded in reality," noting that "people had strong beliefs in and fear about the existence of strange, aged women in the mountain ... these women never wanted to live outside the mountains."[8] Baba finds a clue to the origin of the yamamba in a description Lady Sarashina (the daughter of Sugawara no Takasue, 1008–?) provides of three female entertainers she meets while traveling through Mt. Ashigara as an impressionable twelve-year-old girl. She describes the experience in her memoir, known to us as *Sarashina nikki* (As I Cross a Bridge of Dreams, eleventh century):

> We lodged at the foot of the mountain, and I
> felt fearfully lost in the depth of the moonless
> night. From somewhere in the dark three women
> singers emerged, the eldest being about fifty, the
> others about twenty and fourteen.... Our party
> was charmed by their appearance and even more
> impressed when they started singing, for they had

fine, clear voices that rose to the heavens.... Yes, they
were really pretty to look at, and their beautiful
singing ended far too soon. We were all so sad to see
them disappear into those fearful mountains.[9]

Baba believes that these singers' geographical base was
in the mountain, and they made their living by entertaining
passersby, and she conjectures that once these women grew
old, they continued to live in the mountains, becoming
yamamba.[10] Folklorist Yanagita Kunio provides additional
suppositions for the origin of mountain woman traditions: a
yamamba was believed to exist in the deep mountains both in
the past and in the present (in his case, 1925, when his article
was written), and there were also women who went into the
mountains of their own accord.[11] Yanagita states that these
women were in many cases neurologically challenged (or as he
would have it "insane"); he tells of women who willingly went
into the mountains believing they would become a mountain
deity's bride and, in other cases, of women who wandered into
the mountains after childbirth perhaps due to postpartum
depression. The women whom Lady Sarashina encountered
were living in the mountains of their own volition, though
were certainly not insane. The association between some
yamamba and itinerant dancers is borne out in the earlier
referenced Noh drama.

YAMAMBA'S SEX AND GENDER

As mysterious and contradictory as the yamamba can be, the
overarching key words associated with her are "mountains"
and "femaleness." The yamamba is often conflated with

the female *oni,* or demon. However, the gender of an *oni* is fluid because an *oni* can freely transform itself. The sex of a yamamba, who sometimes is the mother of many children, is always female. Let's turn to a brief explanation of the *oni*'s gender.

An *oni* is popularly portrayed as masculine. I believe that this assumption regarding gender comes primarily from the pictorial representation of *oni*. More often than not, an *oni* is depicted with a muscular body and is scantily clad, wearing a tiger-skin loincloth. The *oni* is hairy and customarily portrayed with one or more horns protruding from its scalp. *Oni* sometimes have a third eye in the center of their forehead and vary in skin color, but most commonly they are black, red, blue, or yellow. They often have large mouths with conspicuous canine teeth.

As I stated earlier, *oni* held no fixed gender and could manifest as either male or female, depending on the circumstances. To complicate the matter further, in the medieval period the label *oni* was even applied to the specters of ordinary household objects, such as tools and containers, after they had reached a hundred years of age. Named *tsukumo-gami,* or animating objects, these abandoned, manmade objects were believed to bear grudges against the people who used and discarded them. Certainly, household objects do not have gender in Japanese. He–she–it, the *oni*, too, is invariably situational and may arguably be considered gender-defiant.

Perhaps there is a curious connection between this fear of long-lived items and the fear of women who have outlived their prime. *Hanayo no hime* (Blossom Princess), a late-sixteenth- or early-seventeenth-century tale, describes a woman––yamamba––who continues to live even after all of her descendants have died. She takes up residence in the mountains with an *oni* as a companion. Although she does not eat humans, she is seen as an *oni* herself by the sheer dint of her longevity.

Compared with the ambiguous gender of an *oni*, a yamamba is and has always been female. The term "female" may invoke a symbolic sense of outsider-ness or the *other*. As Claire R. Farrer observes, the image of women as Other has been a constraining influence on women,[12] especially in patriarchal societies like premodern Japan. The yamamba, however, is much less constrained by the tradition, customs, and social norms expected for a woman.

From the viewpoint of gender studies, Mizuta Noriko says that the yamamba is gender transcendent. She contrasts the yamamba with the women of the village or settlement (*sato*). The village was considered a safe place where people were protected and insulated from the various dangers of the mountains. According to Mizuta, the women of the village are idealized and standardized—they are good mothers, good wives, chaste, humble, and obedient to their fathers and husbands.[13] Conversely, a yamamba is someone who falls distinctly outside of the norm. Although associated with excessive fertility (as represented by her ability to give birth to 7,800 babies at once), she is often depicted as lacking the feminine traits ascribed to the women of the village, namely, chastity, obedience, and compassion. Mizuta notes that the norm for the village women cannot be applied to the yamamba, for her essential qualities are so nebulous and polysemous that she nullifies it.[14] She refuses to be assigned a household role such as mother or daughter and will not be confined.

Mizuta emphasizes that while the women of the village stay in one place, the yamamba is comparatively nomadic, moving constantly through the mountains, appearing in an array of locales, often outside or away from a town's territorial boundary.[15]

YAMAMBA AS GODDESS

A yamamba may be grasped as an archetype that represents the four seasons in nature, as is suggested in the Noh play *Yamamba,* or as a goddess. Yanagita theorized that *yōkai* were deities who had become degraded, i.e., fallen from their status as deities.[16] Following Yanagita's thoughts, Yoshida Atsuhiko, a scholar of mythology, asserts that a yamamba used to be worshiped as a goddess and that the remains of her worship and rites are visible all over Japan.[17]

Komatsu Kazuhiko, an anthropologist and authority on *yōkai* culture, however, warns that this downfall theory is only a supposition, and that the yamamba described in literature and folklore has always possessed a duality of good and evil. A yamamba is characterized by this very duality, and which aspect is emphasized depends on the relation between the yamamba and the individuals or the interests of the time period.[18] Unlike Yanagita Kunio who considers that *yōkai* are deities fallen from grace, Komatsu grasps that worshiped supernatural beings are deities and un-worshipped ones are *yōkai*.[19] One half of the yamamba's genealogy goes back to goddesses, and the other half to *oni*.[20] Indeed, while there are many legends of the yamamba as a mountain deity, she is simultaneously inseparable from an *oni*. It is not that the yamamba fell from the high position she held in ancient Japan and was relegated to the negative side as time passed. She was perceived by contemporary people, at least people in the capital, to be *oni*-like from the beginning of her appearance in the medieval period.

A yamamba encompasses good and evil sides. While the yamamba's roots are found in ancient goddesses, I believe the yamamba is the product of the medieval zeitgeist. For people who were awed and frightened by mountains, strange women in the mountains symbolized manifestations of mountain spirits and the awe accompanying changing seasons. The name and characteristics of the yamamba were creations of the medieval period, amalgamating various elements—both positive and negative—into an archetype.

CONCLUSION

So, who *was* the yamamba? Was she merely a figment of the imagination, a myth derived from the fear of the unknown? Was she the residual creation over time of misogynistic attitudes toward women who dared to live beyond the confines of the village; women who traveled; women who refused to die? The yamamba was all this and more. She was a container for the mysterious power of nature.

Or, perhaps the question might be phrased more accurately, who IS the yamamba? The yamamba is still robust in contemporary Japan. She is depicted in various literary works and media including film and manga. Many still remember vividly (if not fondly) yamamba-like figures such as the *ganguro* (face black girl) whose unique fashion took major cities by storm at the turn of the twenty-first century. A yamamba is a projection of human characteristics with

Japanese desires and fears. What people take out of such multidimensional yamamba depends upon the reader/audience, and that is what makes the yamamba fascinating. Modern and ancient, powerful in their ability to express the human condition, yamamba can always be reimagined.

Yamamba on the Noh Stage: With Noh Actors Uzawa Hisa and Uzawa Hikaru

Ann Sherif

One of the most compelling representations of the yamamba is in the Noh play of the same title. In this interview, acclaimed Noh actors Uzawa Hisa and Uzawa Hikaru discuss their experiences performing Yamamba *and their interpretations of the Noh-inflected representation of yamamba. Noh is a classical theater combining dance and song that dates to the fourteenth century, when it was an art form for the entertainment of military rulers and the gods. Today, Noh continues as one of Japan's living traditional performing arts. The Uzawas' skill and artistry have earned them solid standing at the highest levels of Noh practice as two women in a male-dominated profession. In December 2019, Ann Sherif conducted this interview with the Uzawas, first on their practice stage in Tokyo and later on Skype. (All translations from the play* Yamamba *in the interview below are by Monica Bethe and Karen Brazell from their co-edited* Traditional Japanese Theater. *The interviews were conducted in Japanese and translated by the author.)*

Uzawa Hisa and Uzawa Hikaru dedicate this interview to the memory of Mae Smethurst (1935–2019), scholar of Noh, mentor, and friend.

ANN: How would you describe the Noh play *Yamamba*?

HISA: In Act I, we are introduced to a young dancer named Hyakuma Yamamba. Though she is very famous in the capital for her *kusemai* (storytelling accompanied by dance) about a yamamba, she doesn't want to be complacent and keep doing the same thing again and again. So she decides to go on a pilgrimage to the famous Zenkōji temple in Shinano no kuni (present day Nagano Prefecture). She sets out from the capital with her retainer—I'll call him the manager, since she's a star in the capital. Often in Noh plays, the *waki* (or side) role that interacts with the lead actor is a monk. However, in this play, the audience knows that the *waki* role is not a holy man because the performer is wearing ordinary clothes, instead of a Buddhist monk's robes.

At one point in their long journey, the dancer has to decide which of the several routes that lead to Zenkōji they will take. She chooses the steepest, most challenging path. That means she has to get off the horse, or ox or whatever she was riding, and go the rest of the way by foot. Noh isn't a realistic theater, so we don't see how she is traveling.

HIKARU: Then, as they are making their way up the mountain, it suddenly gets dark.

HISA: They started climbing around midday so they didn't expect it to get dark so soon. "How strange!" Hyakuma Yamamba thinks. Then, from deep in the mountain, they hear a voice saying, "Travelers, it's dark now, so I will accompany you to a place where you can stay." The person speaking appears to be a woman, a woman who lives in these mountains, an older woman.

ANN: In Noh, how does the old woman in the mountains look?

HISA: In the Noh play, the *shite* (main actor) plays the mountain woman, and in Act II the *shite* returns in the form of the yamamba. In Act I, the *shite*'s costume has "no color" (*iro nashi*, meaning no red hues), which indicates that it's not a young woman. The mask in Act I is also that of a middle-aged woman.

To return to the story: The mountain woman tells Hyakuma Yamamba that she made the sky darken so she could offer lodging to them. She wants to hear the dancer's famous yamamba song (*uta*) that she's heard so much about. The text here suggests that she is challenging the entertainer: "You may be a renowned singer and dancer who performs the yamamba. But have you ever *seen* a real yamamba?"

Needless to say, the dancer thinks this is quite unusual. And then, the mountain woman says to her, "I am a real yamamba and here I am before you. Please sing your song for me."

HIKARU: And please clear me of my delusions (*mōshū*).

HISA: Yes, delusion is a major concern in this play.

HIKARU: She says, "If you will sing your song tonight as the moon rises, I will appear in my true form as Yamamba!" And with that, the mysterious woman vanishes. That's the end of Act I.

HIKARU: Immediately following is an interlude (*nakairi*) in which the guide and a local person talk about legends of female demons (*kijo*). In some Noh performances, they talk about what the yamamba is made of, such as nuts, mushrooms, plants, metal, and other substances.

HISA: Early in Act II, the dancer decides that she will sing and dance for the mountain dweller, but she does not in fact sing anything at that point in the play. As the chorus chants about the moon illuminating the sky, the real yamamba appears. There's the question of whether the yamamba looks like a woman or like a man. The *shite* is wearing a wig and is a rather androgynous figure. The gender is not distinct. Even though the yamamba is referred to as a female demon, the figure on stage could be a woman, might be a man. The audience can't tell. It's even less clear to the performer.

ANN: The performer isn't clear whether the yamamba is woman or man?

HISA: We say that it's like the mountain moves and comes out on stage. Yamamba is the mountain, and nature itself. What is important is where the energy comes from, not who the character is. During my lessons, my teacher Kanze Hisao Sensei taught me that the yamamba embodies an unimaginable amount of energy, and that's what the *shite* has to perform. It should be like a mountain moving, which is something extraordinary, beyond our powers of imagination. The performer has to conceive of that level of strength and energy. It's clearly beyond what a human is capable of, so the performer just has to try to the best of her ability. I couldn't just pull it out of my pocket, that's for sure! I found it really challenging, especially when I was young.

ANN: The beginning of Act II features stunning natural imagery of the moon and the mountains.

HISA: Yes, those lines are full of dense natural images, but the text here also is quite philosophical and difficult. "Awesome, the deep ravines/In graveyards, beating their own bones, fiendish wraiths/groan, bemoaning their deeds from former lives ... good and evil are not two ... mountains beyond mountains ... waters beyond waters." These lines evoke the mountain, nature itself.

HIKARU: The mountain embodies this world, which relates both to nature and to Buddhist cosmology.

HISA: When chanting those words, the performer has to blend the many Buddhist ideas in this passage with one's breathing and physical form. It requires a great deal of energy. I find the aesthetic sense in this passage striking. What comes through here is not ordinary beauty but a severe beauty. It's the severity and harshness of nature, not human's notion of harshness. Among the many Noh plays, *Yamamba* particularly challenges the *shite* because of the requirement to perform something vast and transcendent.

ANN: The music in this section is especially energetic and striking.

HISA: The drummers have to put their all into this part; their playing helps to bring alive the chanting of this particular passage. Both of the drums, *otsuzumi* (hip drum) and *kotsuzumi* (shoulder drum), weigh in. So it's very intricately structured. By the same token, the instrumentalists can do that only if the *shite*'s chanting is just right. The *shite* is taking the lead here, not the instrumentalists. So this long passage in the second act is extremely difficult.

ANN: The yamamba is an ambiguous figure. In some legends, she is a demon that eats human flesh. But not in this Noh play.

HISA: That's true. In the part of the play when the young dancer is trying to find out who this mysterious woman is and suspects she might be the yamamba, the dancer is afraid. She grew up hearing the legend of the yamamba as a demon (*oni*) that eats humans. In contrast, the yamamba in the Noh play tells her not to be afraid—she's not that kind of *oni*.

HIKARU: In the text, the dancer says that it's like seeing a demon roof tile for the first time [a common decorative tile similar to a gargoyle], with eyes shining, a red face, and bushy hair, so she does have a frightening appearance. She's also very surprised when she sees the yamamba because the yamamba is able to speak human language.

HISA: Even though the yamamba herself says that she doesn't intend to be scary, the young woman finds her scary.

HIKARU: Then the yamamba presses the dancer to perform the song and dance (*kusemai*).

HISA: *Kusemai* was a distinct performance art that was performed in Zeami's day [nearly seven hundred years ago when he was shaping Noh as we know it today].

HIKARU: The lines in this part mean "Dragging good and evil Yamamba/Makes her mountain rounds in pain."

HISA: These lines impress on us the contrast between the light little songs that Hyakuma Yamamba was singing to entertain her audience and the songs of the real yamamba.

This next passage is very profound. One might expect the play to end here, since Hyakuma Yamamba sang her song for Yamamba, but in this final section the *shite* and chorus chant

HAFUKA SHIGERU

*Uzawa Hikaru as Yamamba (left) and Uzawa Hisa as Hyakuma Yamamba (right)
performing* Yamamba *at the 102nd Annual Kawasaki-shi Teiki Noh, Kawasaki Noh
Theater, Kawasaki, Japan, 2014.*

lines about the vast scale of nature: "Vast and empty valley
voice/Reverberates ... brimming waters of the sea...."

So the play is not only about Yamamba, but also about
nature. Nature is represented here as awesome but also as
the interconnection among all creatures and the non-human
world. Nature is not a threat to humans. In the Noh, Yamamba
is not a malevolent crone. For example, the text says she helps
weaving girls with their backbreaking work. And when once
in a while a woodsman's burden is lightened, it is because
she helps him out. Yamamba says that sometimes she assists
humans, which symbolizes nature's benevolence. I think Japanese views of nature are well represented in this play.

HIKARU: The theme of delusion (attachment that hinders
enlightenment; delusory attachment) comes back in this part

of Act II. Yamamba tells the dancer to "return to the capital/ tell the world these tales." In the same line, Yamamba realizes that her wish to be known in the capital may be spiritually problematic, because it shows she is attached to fame and reputation. She asks herself, "Is this still delusion?"

She's not easy on herself! "Yamamba makes her mountain rounds in pain." Yamamba holds herself to high standards, in Buddhist terms. The text spells this out clearly. She should not be thinking (proudly) about all the things she does to help humans. Thoughts like that are themselves delusions because such thoughts indicate getting caught up in the "self" (jiko). Many Noh plays revolve around the Buddhist notions of delusion. Even though Yamamba possesses supernatural powers, she is still concerned about her spiritual well-being and potential for enlightenment. In many other Noh plays, we see ordinary humans, or their ghosts, who are similarly vexed by delusory attachments and who are therefore stuck in some kind of limbo. Unrequited love, excessive passion, jealousy resulting from being too much in love—these are some of the most familiar tropes concerning delusion in Noh plays. Noh doesn't simply condemn Yamamba's attachment to pride or reputation, but shows her very human, very relatable struggle with her feelings and aspirations, on the one hand, and her spiritual goals, on the other.

HISA: At the very end of the play, Yamamba returns to the mountains. The chanting here uses metaphor to suggest her struggle: "Clouds of delusion scattered and accumulated."

HIKARU: The play constantly brings together opposites and makes them one.

HISA: Recently, I heard a lecture by Professor Haruo Shirane about his book *Japan and the Culture of the Four Seasons*, which describes concepts and representations of nature in classical Japanese literature and the arts. His emphasis on the construction of the four seasons through use of conventional imagery and concepts of the closeness of nature and people is helping me think through what's going on in the play *Yamamba*.

HIKARU: Totally. Toward the end of the play, Zeami uses multiple images of the changing of the seasons and the cycles of the four seasons, year after year, forever and ever. In turn, that cyclical movement of the seasonal change is the endless cycle of birth and rebirth (*rinne*). Even as the poetic language celebrates the beauty and poignancy of the changing seasons, our very emotional and aesthetic attachments to those cycles of nature are themselves delusions, which endlessly accumulate.

HISA: *Yamamba* offers up binarisms but then plays with those and makes them fuzzy. Yamamba is nature, but nature also controls her. There's not really a resolution, because in the end she disappears, somewhere, we don't know where.

HIKARU: I hope audiences will understand that *Yamamba* asks us to imagine on a big scale. It's very philosophical, cosmic. We gave you a really long synopsis of the play!

ANN: I learned a lot from your interpretations and comments on the performance elements. Now for my next question: Is *Yamamba* an important play in the contemporary Noh repertoire?

HISA: Definitely! *Yamamba* is highly valued. It's an

extraordinary play that Noh actors must perform on stage at some point in their career. Performing *Yamamba* well is a true accomplishment, and a rite of passage in the trajectory of a Noh actor's career, particularly in Tessenkai (a branch of the Kanze School of Noh). When I was young, it was especially challenging. You need external and internal strength, physical and spiritual strength, and you use a place deep inside to perform the role of Yamamba. You are performing a mountain. Think about that—how can you move a mountain?

ANN: For someone who's going to see *Yamamba*, what are the high points of the play?

HISA: There's a fair amount of movement in the play. The audience shouldn't be intimidated by the libretto, even though Zeami invokes some heavy philosophical and religious concepts. You can also watch for the dynamics between Hyakuma Yamamba, the young performer, and Yamamba, who is the real thing. When I was young, my teachers, Kanze Tetsunojō IX and Hisao Sensei, helped me understand the play this way. Basically, Hyakuma Yamamba is an idol, a celebrity like Misora Hibari or Yamaguchi Momoe. Oh, am I dating myself here by mentioning singers from so long ago? [Laughter.] So a star sets out on a pilgrimage to a sacred temple and finds herself face to face with the very incredible being that her biggest hit is about—Yamamba! An encounter like that would make any artist stop and think about what it is she's doing when she performs. Even though Hyakuma Yamamba is something of a star in her own time, the Noh play makes clear that we shouldn't underestimate her integrity and depth. After all, she made the choice to step away from the bright lights and to pursue a spiritual goal.

So that's another angle for the audience to think about when watching *Yamamba*. For someone who became famous at a relatively young age, there comes a time when she sits back and takes stock. It's wild, when you think about it, that this girl Hyakuma Yamamba not only meets the real yamamba that she's been singing about, but also sees with her own eyes how awesome she is. The philosophical or religious aspects of the play may be less accessible to audiences, so it's this encounter between a performer and the subject of her performance that makes the play really intriguing.

HIKARU: That's right. Act I includes a relatively long and detailed section about the dancer, before the *shite* even appears on stage. In it, we get a good sense of Hyakuma Yamamba's personality. We learn that, given a choice, she picks the most difficult route [to the temple], and is willing to make the rest of the arduous journey by foot. Zeami wanted the audience to understand her as mature and thoughtful, so he devotes considerable space in the play to evoking her that way. If he hadn't wanted us to get a full sense of her as a person, he would have just made her role much more minor. The *tsure* (companion) role is rarely so prominent in Noh. Even in Act II, Zeami brings Hyakuma Yamamba forward at points.

HISA: I wanted to mention that other versions of *Yamamba* do exist that include an established performance variant called, in this case, "snow moon flowers" (*Yamamba no setsugeka*). This variant is a scene in which Hyakuma Yamamba stands up and actually performs her Yamamba dance with the real yamamba sitting there and watching her. So I think that Zeami wanted the audience to find interest in those contrasts between light and heavy, insubstantial and profound. In other

HAFUKA SHIGERU

Uzawa Hisa, Tessankai Noh Theater, Tokyo, January, 2019.

words, the play isn't just about a yamamba, but also about the dynamic of the dancer encountering her and then performing Yamamba *for* Yamamba.

ANN: Many scholars have analyzed the *kusemai* dance in Act II. Why is there so much attention paid to this section of the play?

HISA: The *kusemai* is fascinating. In contrast to much Noh movement, which tends not to signify what is being described in the text, the *kata* (sequence of movements) in the *kusemai* are fairly concrete. For example, the *kata* with the lines "she shoulders his heavy burden" actually suggest that action. In this part, more than in many Noh plays, the *kata* represents something described in the chanting. It's less abstract than most. The *kusemai* has two relatively long, distinct parts, so you can watch that structure develop over time.

HIKARU: The *kusemai* can stand on its own because of that. Not too long ago, I performed that as *maibayashi* (excerpt of a Noh play with instrumental accompaniment) from *Yamamba*.

HISA: Even if you just see that section, it is satisfying. Even though the performers in a *maibayashi* are wearing black kimono with a crest and *hakama* (pleated trousers) instead of full costume, wig, and mask, the audience responded really positively. I sensed that they felt the mountain moving. It's a tough piece for the performer.

ANN: Twenty-first-century audiences may want to view *Yamamba* from a gender perspective. The word *kijo* (female demon) specifies the gender of the yamamba as female. Would you share your perspective as Noh actors?

HIKARU: I, for one, don't think of her much as "woman" (*onna*).

HISA: It's hard for me to see how the yamamba fits into twenty-first-century concepts of gender.

ANN: Okay, so, how would the play be different if the demon were "man?" Is there any sense of binarisms in these categories of "woman" and "man" in Noh plays? What does "woman" mean in the context of *Yamamba*?

HIKARU: No, a male demon would not work for this play. If it were a mountain man, then it would be lacking in the scale or weight implicit in the demon role

HISA: If it were a male demon, it would lack interest. We've mentioned that one of the themes in *Yamamba* is delusion or excessive attachment. In classical Japanese literature, you find that some of the more compelling and complex characters burdened by attachment are the female characters. But I don't see this as denigrating women.

ANN: In this case, when you say "scale," do you mean the scale or magnitude of archetypal characters in Noh, and in classical literary works like *The Tale of Genji*?

HISA: *Yamamba* doesn't deal with issues of the social roles of women or gender discrimination in a human society. When we perform *Yamamba*, we don't think of it as performing woman (*onna*).

HIKARU: Even for a male actor, they don't think of this role as a "woman." The performer can't conceive of it that way. In Act I, the *shite* role appears in the form of a woman. She is Yamamba manifesting herself in a human form. So people might be conscious of the character as a woman in Act I. I could imagine that the Act I *shite* could appear as a man too. I couldn't tell you why it is a woman and not a man in Act I.

HISA: The power of the literary source texts and literary archetypes may be one reason. Even in ancient Japanese literary texts and the arts, there have been stories of women who hide or take refuge in the mountains. We see that in other Noh plays like *Adachigahara* (The Plain of Adachi), *Kurozuka* (Black Mound), and *Momijigari* (Maple-viewing). There are so many ancient tales about a dancer, or courtesan, who earns favor in the capital and consorts with powerful people. But what happens to her when she falls out of favor, and her moment of glory is over? Characters like that have no choice but to return to their village. Legend has it that, once home, they are forced to live on their own in the mountains, and eventually turn into an *oni*.

There are stories from the Nara period (eighth century) about a young woman coming to the capital all the way from the Tohoku region up north. She is admired as an accomplished dancer and wins the favor of powerful people. When she is no longer young and at the peak of her beauty, she has to return to her village. The people there shun her [because she has not followed a conventional life course] and she has to live on her own, and then the people in the village call her a demon. Doubtless, there were actual women like that historically, who then also appeared in legends. Complex legends about *oni* evolved. The several Noh plays I've mentioned about those women in the mountains represent the social and spiritual complexity of these women who live on the periphery.

So, to return to *Yamamba*, it's possible that this idol singer herself might someday become a yamamba.

HIKARU: I've wondered about that possibility too. The trope of women taking refuge in the mountains was very powerful.

HISA: So it's not strange, and it wouldn't have been unusual for people living in that era. But I really should ask one of the Noh researchers I know whether my interpretation is valid from a scholarly vantage point. Hikaru and I have been speaking today from a performer's perspective. I can say with certainty that, if the yamamba were a man, it would be a very boring play. There's nothing interesting about a male demon.

HIKARU: I agree. It's the only choice for this play.

ANN: How are the masks and costumes for Yamamba chosen?

HISA: You have several options for the *shite*'s mask in Act I.

HIKARU: For the *shite*'s mask in Act I there are only two

choices: a middle-aged-woman's mask (*fukai*), or an ill and frail woman's mask (*yase onna*). For Act II there is a dedicated mask (*senyōmen*) just for Yamamba, so there's no choice. As for costume, Yamamba is quite a complex figure so there is a wider range to choose from.

HISA: There are subtle variations among the Yamamba masks worn in Act II. But as in some other plays, the Act II mask is only used in that play.

The kimono is also coordinated with the mask. If it's the *yase onna* mask, then the costume will be a fairly somber, grandmotherly kimono. But if they are using the middle-aged-woman's mask like *fukai*, then the costume can be a bit sensual, but definitely not flashy. I wanted to mention that there are also choices in how the costume is worn. One would be wearing it more open at the collar normally. Another is called *ubazuke*, with the collar more somberly drawn close together.

But you can choose how you wear the costume. You can wear it open over the chest like this [Hisa points to the costume in a photograph of her performance], or wear it folded close to the neck. One looks a bit more "feminine," if I may use that term, and the other is androgynous, or rather does not indicate the specific gender of the wearer. When I performed *Yamamba* for the first time, I wanted to wear the costume with the outer robe more open at the chest, but my teacher at the time said, because you are a woman, you should wear it the other way. I did not like the way the costume looked. Back then, there were some people who treated me that way "because you are a woman."

But enough about me! You were asking about what the

performer wears for *Yamamba*. There are kimono motifs associated with demons such as the "checkered triangles" (scales, or *uroko*). Usually we use the yamamba wig. Most yamamba wigs are salt and pepper, or sometimes a big imposing white headpiece associated with female demons.

HIKARU: There is also a dedicated wig called *yamamba gashira* that is brownish.

HISA: I think the *yamamba gashira* is a more recent invention.

ANN: Why does Yamamba help the woodcutter and the weavers? She doesn't have to.

HISA: [Laughing.] No one has ever asked me that before! How should I explain this? Okay, so the hard-working weaver, or the woodsman with his heavy bundle, they feel their burden lifted and think, "Yamamba is helping me." What's being evoked here is not that Yamamba is a superhero who comes to help them. That's not it at all! This passage has to do with nature, which may be threatening but also helps people naturally. But mountains are also awesome.

HIKARU: Yamamba isn't a heroic character.

HISA: When the woodcutter and the weaver feel that way, they associate Yamamba with those feelings of relief. Like when the sun goes down, that's the workings of nature. When you think that something feels different, something's out there, you imagine that might be Yamamba. People made Yamamba out of their imagination.

ANN: Do performances of *Yamamba* vary much among different Noh schools?

HIKARU: Not really. Every school considers it a formidable piece.

One time I watched a performance of *Yamamba* by another Kanze School actor. He was putting a lot of energy into the performance, but I wasn't very impressed. Performing *Yamamba* doesn't mean you just dance as hard and as powerfully as you can. There's more to it than just physical strength. The real challenge for the performer is the relationship between the inner and outer. There are plays that differ noticeably in the ways that schools perform them, but *Yamamba* isn't one of those. But, I really have to ask people in other schools to find out how they do it differently.

ANN: Hikaru-san, have you performed *Yamamba*?

HIKARU: Not as a full Noh play. Earlier, I mentioned performing the featured solo dance of Act II. That was in November 2019 at the Kita Noh Theater in Tokyo. The program included my *Yamamba* solo excerpt, followed by a comic Kyōgen performance. The Noh play was my mother's performance of *Yugyō yanagi* (The Priest and the Willow).

ANN: Were you the one who chose to do *Yamamba* as part of the program?

HIKARU: In determining the program, the Noh play is chosen first, and then you pair it with an appropriate solo excerpt. The Noh play for the program featured a type of dance called *jo no mai*, so we wanted to avoid doing the same type of dance for the solo. Before that, I performed *Yamamba* once a long time ago when I was in my twenties. So I guess this was the second time.

ANN: Is there anything in particular you focus on during practice for *Yamamba?*

HIKARU: During the rehearsal, I was being way too energetic and my pacing was overly deliberate. My mother told me I looked as if I were saying, "look how good I am." You don't want to look like you have gone all crazy technical. So in my 2019 performance, I changed my approach to performance.

ANN: Were you satisfied with the performance?

HIKARU: People in the audience told me they liked it. Even so, I found *Yamamba* to be quite challenging. The strength has to come from within. I felt much more confident the second time I performed it.

ANN: Is it your goal to perform the full play *Yamamba?*

HIKARU: Yes, absolutely. I like the chanting and the text a lot. I know how difficult it will be but I will definitely learn a lot. Is that the right tactic? Should one perform *Yamamba* to learn? Or aim for it even though I know it's a stretch for me? I want to be competent and confident in my chanting skills. Our theater, Tessenkai, regards *Yamamba* as a key play in the repertoire. If I told my teacher that I want to perform it, I'm guessing he'd say yes. I am not sure! [Laughing.] In fact, I'm not at all sure about how he would react if I said I wanted to try *Yamamba.* I've heard that some of my *senpai*—in this case, older male colleagues—have been asking his permission to do *Yamamba.* Even though they are three or four years older than me, Sensei turned them down! By the same token, there are people my age who have already performed *Yamamba,* so it just depends. At Tessenkai, if Sensei doesn't think it will come together, he won't give you the go ahead. But I think it's always good to think you want to do it. It's good to work toward *Yamamba*. I hope I can perform it at some significant time. I want to do it when I'm in my forties.

ANN: Has the relationship between teacher and *deshi* (student) in Noh changed much between your mother's generation and your generation of Noh actors?

HIKARU: The *shite* chooses the mask she will wear. But when you are a young performer, you wait for your teacher to advise you on the choice of mask. There are certain precious masks that only actors with a long record of performance and experience are allowed to wear. A young person might own a certain mask, or have it in her own family, but would not dare use it. You must attain a certain level of ability before you can wear the most valued masks. Even if a young actor did put on such a splendid mask, she would lack the experience and artistry to make effective use of the mask. Thinking modestly is key. This can be seen in expressions like "he's losing to the mask" (*omote ni makete iru*) or "the costume defeats him." You don't want other actors to say that about you so it's better to hold back.

HISA: If, one day, the sensei takes out a fine mask and says you can use it, you know you're being recognized. In those days, you would never ask your teacher to be allowed to use a fine mask. Now, there are some young people who ask their sensei to use a certain mask. We *senpai* look askance at that. Hikaru would never ask to use a mask.

Here are two photos of my performances of *Yamamba*. My first performance was March 28, 1993—the 19th Annual

Hakujukai, at the Kanze Noh Theater, which was in Shibuya in those days. I remember it as very challenging. I wore the *yamamba gashira* wig, which is brown mixed with blond. For this first performance, I wore the *yase onna* mask. The second photo is of my September 14, 2014, performance, the 102nd Annual Kawasaki City Noh. In Act I, I used the *yase onna* mask, both in this and the first performance. For Act II, I wore a white wig, per the variant performance (*kogaki*), and a yamamba mask we have at home. The first time I wore a mask was at the Kanze Theater, and the facial expression is slightly different. Hikaru played the *tsure* role that time. This was a production with variation in which the Hyakuma Yamamba and the real Yamamba are dancing together. I was about forty-four at the time.

HIKARU: Really? Then I will perform *Yamamba* when I'm forty-four too.

ANN: The great theorist and playwright Zeami proposed stages in a Noh actor's career, which is roughly a lifetime. How does *Yamamba* fit into this trajectory that Zeami proposed?

HISA: When I was in my mid-forties, trying to do such a demanding piece was hard. So the second time was easier in some ways, but even then I was trying to access strength that I didn't have. And the second time, it went well, but it was still formidable. As a Noh actor ages, sustaining physical strength and endurance rather than technique becomes the focus. Expressivity is important too of course.

Zeami wrote that the last phase of an actor's career starts around age fifty. In Zeami's time, people's life expectancy was much shorter so fifty was late in life. Even though I'm older

Formal Portrait of Uzawa Hikaru (2015).

than that now, I am around that last stage of a Noh performer's career that Zeami wrote about in his treatise. Even so, I keep challenging myself. If one becomes complacent or self-satisfied, that's a problem.

ANN: For my final question, what would you like to highlight about *Yamamba* to your English-language readers?

HISA: I hope our readers will pay attention to the attitudes toward nature expressed in the Noh play *Yamamba*, and the ways people have co-existed with nature. Also how much strength the performance demands.

HIKARU: Even if you're not Japanese, everyone should have that sense about nature. But I do recommend that people learn something about the play before they see it.

HISA: One other thing that's important to keep in mind is that Noh demands a lot of its audience. In particular, Noh relies on the audience members engaging with their imagination as they watch the stylized performance on the minimalist stage. In Act II of *Yamamba*, the lines "Awesome, the deep ravines/In graveyards, beating their own bones, fiendish wraiths/groan, bemoaning their deeds from former lives/In cemeteries, offering flowers/angelic spirits/rejoice in the good rewards of enlightened acts" are a kind of abstract conversation. I remember thinking as I was performing this section about a surrealist painting I'd seen somewhere. The painting shows a hut, and a skeleton on the ground in the foreground. It's mostly black and white. The words in this part are like that painting, where there's no color.

Right after the rather dark passage I quoted just now about "wraiths beating their bones," the text suddenly mentions "angelic spirits" who offer flowers as a way of rejoicing "in the good rewards of enlightened acts." It makes me think in full color, bright, and gold. I really like this passage. It's incredibly difficult to perform but I still like it. When you're performing or practicing this, you really have to use your imagination. You can't be just repeating the lines. Pictures can help you imagine what is going on in a passage. I go quite often to museums to see paintings. I'm fond of Western music too. I want to connect what I'm doing on stage to my own artistic sensibility, while at the same time inspiring the audience to engage with their artistic imagination and experiences with the arts.

Connecting Noh with the visual arts and other media can be useful. Here is another passage from *Yamamba* that is fantastic: "Mountain beyond mountains (*yama mata yama*)/

Whose skill sculpted those azure cliffs?/Waters beyond waters (*mizu mata wa mizu*),/In whose house were their jade colors dyed?" So you can imagine that the scene being evoked here is rocky, maybe without vegetation and cold black and white. Trees might not be growing but there is water in the deep valleys, the green and the beautiful blue of the water. The contrasts are fantastic, and it fits perfectly with the rhythms. A fabulous piece! And you are standing there alone and you look out to the right, and chant, "*yama mata yama*" (mountains beyond mountains).

My father demonstrated the right way to chant "*yama mata yama*" for me. You can't just sing it smoothly, but instead you have to draw out and exaggerate the *ma* of *yama*. [At this point in the interview, Hisa starts chanting again, and then comments, "This part is SO hard!"]. The breathing and chanting are coordinated well with the meaning of the words. This part is difficult but it feels worth it because it is so skillfully written.

ANN: Thank you for the interview. I've learned a lot.

HIKARU: It's been a pleasure.

HISA: You've asked us some questions that made us think in new ways about *Yamamba*.

Noh actor UZAWA HISA was born into a Noh family and is a member of the Tessenkai branch of the Kanze School Noh Theater. Her father and first teacher Uzawa Masashi was *shite-kata* (lead actor) in the Kanze Tessenkai School. She also studied with pioneering Noh actor Kanze Hisao and head of the Tessenkai School, Kanze Tetsunojō X. She debuted on the Noh stage at the age of three, and her first performance as *shite* was at the age of thirteen. She earned a degree from the Tokyo University of Arts and Music. In addition to milestone plays in a Noh actor's career such as *Dōjōji*, Uzawa

Hisa regularly performs a wide range of Noh plays in theaters throughout Japan and abroad and has appeared in modern theater productions such as *Oedipus* and *Chieko shō* (Portrait of Chieko). For her achievements as a Noh performer and educator, Uzawa Hisa was awarded the Kawasaki City Cultural Prize (2005) and the prestigious 40th Kanze Hisao-Hosei University Noh Theater Prize (2018).

UZAWA HIKARU, Hisa's daughter, is also a member of the Tessenkai branch. She has trained under such masters of the Kanze School as her own mother and grandfather, the late Uzawa Masashi, and the head of Tessenkai, Kanze Tetsunojō IX. At the age of three, Uzawa Hikaru made her first stage appearance in the Noh play *Oimatsu* (The Old Pine Tree), and since then she has continued to promote the tradition as one of the handful of female Noh actors. She has been involved in numerous Noh performances including *Shakkyō* (Stone Bridge), *Midare* (The Tipsy Elf), and *Dōjōji* (Dōjō Temple) in Japan, and overseas in the U.S., Canada, Norway, Australia, Poland, and Brazil. Uzawa Hikaru collaborates in Nanjing and Hong Kong on performances combining Noh with contemporary theater and dance, as well as other traditional performing arts from around the world. A graduate of Tokyo University of Arts and Music with a major in Noh Theater, Uzawa Hikaru teaches Noh at Rikkyō University and Senzoku University of Music, Tokyo.

Yamamba's Mountains
山姥の山巡り

Linda C. Ehrlich, Japanese translation by Ohmori Kayo

Yamamba
Old woman of the mountain
emerges from darkness,

dragging the seasons behind.

山姥
山に棲む老婆
暗闇から現れる
季節を引き摺り込む

Silently she strengthens the hand of the weaver

Yamamba of the carpenters,
Yamamba of the filtered forest light.

音もなく、山姥は機織りの手を強くする
木こり達の
山姥
森から漏れる澄んだ光

Around her all is awakening.

In the break in the flowering branches—

that too is Yamamba
reaching down.

山姥の周りでは、すべてのものが目を覚ます

花の咲いた枝にも、
山姥は手を伸ばす

What is beyond understanding
must be understood.
What is understood
must never be forgotten.

理解の及ばないものを
理解しなければならない。
理解したものは
決して忘れない。

Yamamba gathers her rags around her body
like wild sorrel.

Stamping like thunder!

山姥は　自分のぼろ布を身体中に纏い
まるで野生植物のよう.

山姥
雷のように足を踏み鳴らす！

Morning sun turns the hills
smoky
with striated light.

朝の太陽は、光の縞をふり注いで
丘を煙らせる

Old woman of the mountain,
emerges from darkness,
    leaning on her evergreen cane

山に棲む老婆
暗闇から　あらわれる
　　常緑の杖に身を傾けて

and enters again

the blinding

morning
　light.

そして再び
朝の眩しい光の中へ
入り込んでいく

Blue Ridge Yamamba

Rebecca Copeland

I was surprised to see a woman there, on the other side of the stream. She was kneeling on the rocky bank peering into one of the temporary pools left by a stray rivulet. Her long gray hair hung loose over her face, threatening to dip into the water if she crouched any lower. I couldn't tell if she was looking at something in the pool, or at her own reflection.

She was on private property. My property. I hadn't seen any vehicle parked along the road where I'd entered the woods, half a mile up the mountainside, and had no idea where she'd come from. I watched her for a moment, perplexed. It was late August and the trees were still thick with leaves. What with my screen of greenery and her mop of hair, I didn't think she could see me.

"You're wondering why I'm here, aren't you?"

It wasn't exactly that she spoke to me. She was too far away and the water in the stream too loud for her voice to have been so distinct. It sounded as if she were right beside me. Or more like the voice came from inside my own head. I felt a shiver slip down my spine. The rock I was standing on gave way at that moment and I slid a few inches down the steep path, landing momentarily on my backside before regaining my footing. When I looked again, she was gone.

After I returned to my cabin overlooking Three Top Mountain, I began to doubt that I had seen anyone. It had been close to dusk. Perhaps my mind had played tricks. My mother had just died, and I was feeling lonely, searching for her traces everywhere I turned. This had been her cabin, the one she and my father had purchased as their weekend refuge. My father died; and then three years later she died, too. My sisters and I carried her clothes and things from the cabin to the local thrift shop. But her traces remained in the random scraps of paper I came across unexpectedly, wedged in a drawer or tucked in the pages of a book: handwritten recipes, Bible verses, affirmations and reminders. Each time I discovered one, I would slip back in time, feeling as if she were there beside me. Her penmanship was neat, clear, and gently tilted. In comparison, my notes were a scrawled mess. And yet, there was something similar in them too. The forward tilt, perhaps? Hers was soft and elegant. Mine seemed to rush to the end of the page.

There was a place in the woods that similarly bore her imprint, and that was where I was headed when I came across the old woman. Mother had created a sanctuary deep beneath a stand of hemlocks ringed with feathery ferns. When she found a moment to herself, which was rare, she retreated there to reflect and dream. I never asked her of what she dreamed. I never troubled myself too much with my mother's inner life. Could the vision by the stream have been a projection of my loss? An old woman peering into the pool of her past? But there was nothing about that wild-looking gray-haired vision that even remotely resembled my late mother, who had gone without fail every three weeks to have her hair set at Miss Phoebe's Beauty Salon.

※

Three days later I was sitting on my porch overlooking the blue-layered sweep of mountains and enjoying the breeze coming up from the valley. The early afternoon sun shone bright on the nodding yellow wildflowers in the meadow below the cabin. When it got a little cooler, I planned to creep down over the stones to cut a few of the flowers for the kitchen table. They never lasted long, but they brought me pleasure in the short term. A pair of black butterflies danced lightly over the field, soaring up above the petals with wings entwined before separating and landing lightly on the blooms. They made it seem so effortless, the dance of love, the pairing. Somehow it had never worked for me. I'd come to the cabin, not to commune with my mother's spirit—though that had become a happy consequence—but to escape the vitriol that had become my twenty-year marriage. The slamming doors and breaking glass were disturbing, but worse was the leaden silence that followed. I had to leave, clear my head, think. I did not want to divorce. At fifty-seven, I was too old now to start over. I'd just have to work it out, turn down the promotion that seemed to irritate him, and spend more time at home. But the thought of tiptoeing about, so as not to annoy a man whose nerves were always taut, left me feeling helpless.

Our marriage had not always been miserable, of course. We had once entwined with delight—like the fluttering butterflies—soaring, sparking, our hearts beating so madly they nearly bruised our ribs. The passion was magnificent. But it was the quiet that followed that ensnared me. I remember lying naked next to him in our rumpled bed, our bodies spent, sighing contentedly as the sweat on our necks and bellies evaporated. Drifting off to sleep, I would feel him gently pull the sheet over my hips as I lay curled in his embrace, his breath damp on my shoulders. The memory was now distant. He claimed he had lost the ability to have sex. First it was a groin pull suffered on his package-delivery job. Then it was a slipped disk that was never quite bad enough to demand medical attention, and finally he professed depression. At first I showered him with sympathy, going out of my way to make sure he was comfortable—offering to bring him warm toddies before bed or massage his back. I was patient. I waited, lying sleeplessly beside him counting his breaths. This was what marriage was, after all, the silent sharing of each other's pain. After two years passed and then three, it finally dawned on me that he was not abstaining from sex. He was abstaining from me. By then, I had grown used to my involuntary celibacy, grateful even to have a man who came home to me. I grew fat. I stopped caring.

The skies suddenly darkened. It was still midday, but the light had faded and black clouds roiled above the valley, erasing the mountain ridgeline. Crows now perched where the butterflies had been, their cobalt wings winking ominously in the mists, and just behind them I could barely see the black garments of an old woman; the same old woman I had seen at the stream. She stood facing me, her silver hair splayed out over her shoulders. Tree limbs rustled, and the black garment billowed around her like a sail. She was wearing a kimono.

"Why shouldn't I wear a kimono?"

She was at least thirty feet away, but her voice was so

distinct, I thought she was standing next to me. In fact, I could almost feel her breath on my face, smell it. Dankly moist, it was not a pleasant smell.

"Do you still not know who I am?"

I shook my head and opened my mouth but the words caught. It felt as if cold fingers gripped my throat. My breath grew thick and labored. I pressed my eyes shut as tightly as I could and opened them again, hoping she would be gone. She wasn't. I could hear her laughing now, a dry raspy rattle.

"You do, though. You know who I am."

I had no idea who she was. Or what she was. Or how. I slowly pulled myself up out of my chair and edged toward the door of the cabin, my knees shaking so loudly I could hear the bones knock.

"I am the yamamba."

She spoke directly in my right ear. I swerved to look at her but there was no one there. A wavering of black fabric caught my eye. She was standing now just beneath the deck, her neck craned back to look up at me. The skin on her throat was paper thin and crepey. Her lips were curled back to reveal long, yellow teeth.

"Scared? Don't be."

Her words only made my terror greater. I reached behind me, grabbing the smooth roundness of the doorknob. I twisted, pushed, and tumbled inside the cabin, slamming the door behind me so sharply that the clear glass panes on the upper half rattled. I turned the lock in the knob and pulled the curtains across the glass. The breath I had been holding leaked out in a long anguished groan.

When I turned toward the kitchen, she was there, a sponge in her hand, wiping down the countertop.

"You really ought to be more tidy, what with the mouse problem you've been having lately." She looked up at me and winked.

I looked quickly over her shoulder, perplexed as to how she had made her way in. Was there a hidden door I didn't know about?

"The yamamba doesn't need a door, you know."

What on earth was she saying? The yamamba, or mountain witch, was a character out of Japanese folklore. I should know, I was a professor of Japanese mythology and had just completed a long study on the origins and attributes of the yamamba. Her aspects were contradictory and inconsistent: she was a demon and a goddess; she cannibalized travelers (mostly men) and eased the burdens of the weary. In my classes at the university my students expressed frustration over her lack of clarity. "Is she good or bad?" they demanded, as if life were ever so black and white. I had tried to explain to them that the yamamba—with all her complexities— suggested the fear early cultures had harbored for independent women, women who thrived beyond the borders of the community, women who refused to be labeled. "Why is it always the woman who is scary?" one of my more sophisticated students had asked. "Why is it that single men are eligible bachelors while women are crazy cat ladies?"

"But, women without men *are* terrifying, aren't they?" the yamamba said, intruding on my thoughts.

What?

"Well, isn't that what you think? Hags, witches! Far better to be a dried-up old sardine of a wife than a woman alone?"

Are you saying I am not independent? I have my own career, and a very successful career it is.

What on earth was I doing arguing with this wraith of a woman? For all I knew, she was just a function of the mist, a figment of my imagination. Besides, what was a Japanese yamamba doing in the Blue Ridge Mountains?

"Why shouldn't I be in the Blue Ridge? Do you think something as flimsy as a national border could stop the yamamba?"

Well, I suppose a yamamba wouldn't need a passport, but there is the matter of the ocean. How did you cross such a wide expanse?

"Nothing contains a yamamba, nothing. We slip through time, we slide through space; with our hands we knead the earth; with our breath we conjure the clouds. We are everywhere and nowhere. We are seen and unseen."

Maybe so, but you also have the reputation for eating men. Don't you think that's kind of disgusting?

"Silly woman. The only thing I eat is fear."

I swallowed hard, trying to fight back the fact that I was terrified of this madwoman in my kitchen.

"I know you're afraid. It's easy for you to stand before your students and lecture them about your feminist views, using the yamamba as your model. But you're afraid of me now, aren't you? You aren't so unlike the others, you know. How they tremble when they see me tearing along the ridgeline. How they try to deny my appetite and trick me into satiety. They stuff my mouth with stones; they fill my gullet with oil. They would have me silent and still or dead. Just like you, living mummy that you are. But I will not keep to the village, the city, the castle, the church, a husband's bed. I will run through the mountains, my robes asunder, my mouth agape. I will devour their terror as I feast on my own freedom."

She raised her long black sleeve and spun it around her head. She was gone.

✳

Five months passed and I returned to the mountain cabin for the winter holidays. There was snow on the roadways, and the drive up had been slow and nerve-wracking. After a quick dinner of Campbell's tomato soup, I put on my pajamas, wrapped a quilt around my shoulders, and stepped out onto the porch to enjoy the moon. The stars, splashed across the dark heavens, were enchanting. I lay back on the rough wooded planks of the decking and looked into the vastness above me, savoring my solitude. I had done it. I had left my husband—not that he had really noticed—and had tendered my resignation at the university. From the spring, I would live here year round. The stars grew brighter, almost as if they were rushing to me. I felt something brush my face, cold and soft. The stars had transformed into eyes, their silver rays now haloed the head of the yamamba. She was hovering just above my face, peering down at me. Smiling. Her teeth were like pearls, smooth and round. She reached out and touched my brow with her finger, gently drawing loops across my skin in an elegant tilt.

Startled, I rolled onto my side, and as I struggled to rise, the yamamba guided me upward with her hands; they were firm and warm. Standing face to face to her, she was taller than me. That surprised me. And she was younger than I had imagined. Her skin was free of wrinkles and nearly luminescent. Her robes too seemed to glow with an uncanny light. Instead of the tattered black sleeves I had seen earlier, her kimono was a serene blue, like the color at the center of a glacier.

"Let's dance!" she laughed. And I could hear music spilling out from the cabin. I didn't remember turning on my iPod. But there was Brandi Carlile's "Every Time I Hear That Song." The yamamba pulled me by the hand and gave me a spin, her arm spiraling over my head. The quilt cascaded from my shoulders and puddled on the porch at our feet. The yamamba adroitly stepped over it and spun me around again. She dipped under my arm and spun herself in the opposite direction, her kimono sleeves billowing out beside her like frozen mist. We spun and spun until I grew dizzy and collapsed on the decking. I looked up and the stars spun around me in a silver ring. I could see my breath rising above me in white puffs. When I turned to look for her, the yamamba was gone.

I knew she would be.

A Yamamba Shrinebox

Laura Miller

Through a mixed-media collage, I am celebrating the yamamba with a few selected objects and images in "A Yamamba Shrinebox."

What is a shrinebox? It is a genre of assemblage folk art with Mexican and South American roots similar to a shadow box. One type is the *retablo*, a frame or shelf enclosing decorated panels or revered objects. Three-dimensional or recessed *retablo* displays were originally meant to commemorate the Virgin Mary, a saint, or a sacred event. A popular incarnation is the Mexican Day of the Dead dioramas called *cajitas de muertos* (skeleton boxes). Day of the Dead shrineboxes might show lively skeleton figures dancing at a fiesta, baking enchiladas, playing cards, or doing other mundane activities. The art evolved to depict secular themes as well.

There are centuries of yamamba representation in art and theater, so I thought she was a good candidate for taking center stage in shrinebox art. I began by searching for images of her to inspire my own interpretation and ideas about her. Numerous drawings and prints depict her as an enticing young woman. A woodblock print by Kitagawa Utamaro (1753–1806) shows a yamamba combing her hair while her son Kintarō clings to her back.[1] Her voluptuous body and milk-gorged breasts are not at all repellent. Artists in the Edo period (1603–1868) loved to use the sexy yamamba as a motif, representing her as a vibrant widow with black hair and pale skin. Young, alluring, and maternal yamamba were popular in stories, prints, and the Bunraku puppet theater.

In contrast, other common depictions of yamamba portray a hideous old woman in ragged clothing wandering in the mountains. The yamamba is often considered to be a type of *yōkai*, a classification used for miscellaneous goblins, ghosts, and other supernatural beings. She is a tricky character who may do evil things to humans. Conversely, she may also at times be quite benign and helpful. These disheveled yamamba always depressed me, as I never thought that there was anything wrong with a woman wanting to flee social pressures and sexist gender norms by escaping into the mountains. One task I set for my art project was to represent yamamba in a more positive manner. I decided to retain the crone motif but to also make her cute and approachable. I don't think old age for women should be viewed as a bad thing.

I noticed that much of the art representing the yamamba draws from a Noh play attributed to Zeami Motokiyo (1363–1443).[2] The play told a story about a supernatural old woman who meets a dancer who performs the role of the mountain hag. In their description of the play, Monica Bethe and Karen Brazell wrote:

> She is an enigma: a god, a demon, an entertainer, a mother; she is enlightened, tormented, helpful, and harmful. Capitalizing on this ambivalence, the noh

LAURA MILLER, MAY 2020

Yamamba Shrinebox with Yamamba-chan on the left, Yamamba Kogyaru in the background to the right, and Yamamba-chan's companion creatures in the foreground.

adds new dimensions to the character of Yamanba. It highlights questions of appearance, reality, and art by introducing an entertainer who impersonates Yamanba to the real Yamanba, who in turn entertains her impersonator.[3]

There is a range of Noh masks used by the actors who perform the part of the yamamba. Some are quite disturbing, presenting a tortured, stern face with a grimace. The mask is usually paired with an enormous wig of long tangled white hair. When I saw Yokoshi Yasuko's performance event *Yamamba Festival* in 2019, the artist who performed the role of the yamamba dancer (as derived from Zeami's play) was a member of the artistic collective known as Dumb Type and was modeled after this motif because she wore the enormous white wig to great effect.

I wanted to incorporate the signifier of the crone's white hair, but the distorted, terrifying face of the mountain ogress found in so many woodblock prints and theater turned me off. Perhaps I could pair an old woman framed with an enormous halo of puffy unkempt white hair with a sweet, adorable face? For my main shrinebox yamamba figure, I decided to represent her as advanced in age, yet wearing a grand kimono suitable for a younger woman, albeit one stained in order to appear muted by time. The fresh doll kimono I purchased was bright and garish. I dipped it in coffee to muddy its hues, so that the original bright lavender is a darker purple, and the bright pink is mauve. The merry face, made from a dried apple, alludes to the subversive potential of the yamamba figure and offers a positive aspect of her persona that I wanted to emphasize. As I worked I began to call her "Yamamba-chan." *Chan* is a form of the name suffix *-san* for Miss, Mrs., or Mr., which denotes endearment or intimacy.

I added a jaunty black-and-white-striped scarf to Yamamba-chan's outfit. I got the idea from watching a Japanese TV series named *Osen*.[4] The story takes place at a high-end multi-course *ryōtei* restaurant named Isshōan. Handa Sen, nicknamed Osen, is the quirky young proprietor. She is a master chef, gardener, potter, and art connoisseur. She inherited the shop from her mother and retains respect for refined food preparation and for the boutique shops and distributors who provide fresh bean curd, dried bonito, and other artisan foodstuffs. She always wears kimono properly, but usually pairs retro and 1920s-era kimono with a textured wool scarf. I loved her irreverent style and understood it as one strategy to complicate her placement in rigid class and gender hierarchies. The yamamba, of course, goes beyond wearing unconventional kimono accoutrements by rejecting regimented community life altogether. But I liked the scarf as a symbol of individuality and a "sod off" attitude. To complete Yamamba-chan's ensemble she is holding a tacky *uchiwa* fan with a painting of a woman straight from an Edo-period woodblock print. I've never seen an image of yamamba holding an *uchiwa*, perhaps because the coolness of the mountains renders them unnecessary. But this stylish Yamamba-chan has her own logic.

The yamamba is always associated with the wild areas of the landscape not monitored by village busybodies. She is usually found roaming the mountains or living in caves or huts in obscure locations. I considered adding a small hut to the shrinebox but did not want to detract attention from Yamamba-chan herself. I added some mountain and forest imagery but thought that adding wild and supernatural creatures would allude to the locale, and also do other symbolic work. Some tales attribute supernatural powers to the yamamba, such as the ability to make the day appear darker or to work as hard as five young men. I illustrate her exceptional supernatural power by including animals and supernatural beings who perceive her as irresistible and as fellow outcasts from normalcy. They long to be in her company. These animals and other companions join her in the mountains.

There is a generic light-gray Bambi-like deer, content to be in Yamamba-chan's circle. A bright yellowish-orange deer named Shikamaro-kun cheerfully stands at attention. Sacred deer are abundant in the former capital of Nara, where they roam freely through the parks and streets. The deer have no fear of humans and actively solicit crackers. In tourism materials Nara is celebrated as the home of these sacred deer. In an effort to boost tourism and local identity branding, many towns and cities in Japan began to create novel mascots or characters that are used for promotional materials, regional signs, stationery, events, and souvenirs. There is even an annual national contest to select the year's favorite mascot. Nara Prefecture has at least sixty mascots created by local civic groups, schools, museums, and other organizations. Unsurprisingly, many of the mascots in Nara feature iconic deer figures. One is the controversial and bizarre Sento-kun, a freakish combination of a deer and a baby Buddhist monk created in 2010. The majority of people in Nara thought Sento-kun was absurd and creepy, so in response many groups put forward alternative mascots. The Nara City Tourist Association created their own official deer mascot, the appealing, chubby deer character Shikamaro-kun. This mascot adorns notebooks, postcards, coffee mugs, and other goods. The two deer hanging out with Yamamba-chan let us know she can't be all bad.

I imagine that Yamamba-chan would also be loved by the fox, itself a creature from mythology with supernatural abilities.[5] Similar to yamamba, the fox, or *kitsune*, is another type of *yōkai* able to shapeshift into human form, most often that of an attractive young woman. I found a realistic model of a brownish-orange fox who now cuddles next to her. Another *kitsune*-like figure was added as well. It is a tan and brick-colored figurine of a cat dressed in a fox costume from a line of collectibles named Furrybones that was designed by Sawada Misaki. Sawada was born in Japan but created the concept and designs for more than one hundred Furrybone characters for a Los Angeles–based company named Pacific Trading (formerly YTC Summit). I liked the *guro-kawaii* (grotesque cute) aesthetic and the ambiguity of this Furrybone cat who is dressing up or "cosplaying" as a fox. "Cosplay," which has now been firmly borrowed into English, is from the Japanese term *kosupure* (itself a clipped form of the borrowed English "costume play"). Costume playing refers to the wearing or adoption of the physical traits, clothing, or accoutrements of well-known characters from folklore, history, or media. The layered meanings of the figure remind me of the multiple and shifting meanings of the yamamba.

Another *yōkai* in the shrinebox mix is a reclining *kappa* made of clay. The *kappa* is a figure from folklore with numerous regional names and variations, but commonly drawn as green and frog-like with a tortoise carapace and beaked mouth.[6] *Kappa* are known as tricksters who might torment and kill humans, primarily by pulling them under water and drowning them. Alternatively, much like yamamba, they might simply assist or prank humans in harmless ways. *Kappa* imagery dates back centuries ago and includes diverse types of supernatural beings, but the majority of them depict a hideous hybrid humanoid amphibious creature. In recent decades the *kappa* has been shown as ultra-cute and turned into a merry mascot and media personality. The shrinebox *kappa* is a subdued cute one, beige and with a brown shell and black eyes. *Kappa* normally live near the rivers, ponds, and wetlands of the valleys and coastlines rather than in the mountains where the yamamba roams. But Yamamba-chan attracts even *kappa* to her entourage. *Kappa* traveled high into the mountains to be with her.

Other humans pity the yamamba living alone in the

mountains, but in fact she is not alone as she has *kappa*, deer, and *kitsune* companions. Two additional figures complete her menagerie. One is a small, hybridized figurine that draws on imagery related to a beloved Buddhist figure named Jizō, who is the Japanese version of the bodhisattva Kṣitigarbha.[7] Bodhisattva are divine beings who deny their own ascension to Buddhahood in order to help others along the path to enlightenment. Jizō often takes the form of a childlike monk who assists the souls of deceased children and others who are traveling or in transition. Jizō might carry a staff or wear a child's bib. The figure in the yamamba shrinebox is from a set of tiny capsule toys delivered from a small crank-style vending machine named *gashapon*. The Gashapon Ojizō-san set includes animals and supernatural beings dressed as Jizō, including a mouse, frog, wild boar, cat, *tanuki*, and fox, all of them in a granite color to allude to their usual status as stone statues. The cosplaying bunny in the shrinebox adds more diversity to the group. Thus, there are two cosplaying animals in the shrinebox—the bunny Jizō and the cat *kitsune*. Is Yamamba-chan also doing cosplay with her elaborate kimono and charming face? The unexpected *uchiwa* may be a clue, or else it simply reflects her sense of humor.

A final addition to the shrinebox assemblage is a tiny replica of a well-known ancient clay burial figurine called a *haniwa*.[8] Molded from terracotta clay, *haniwa* were formed into the shapes of people, animals, tools, musical instruments, and dwellings. Archaeologists have found them at earthen tumuli called *kofun* that date from the beginning of the third century. They were placed inside tombs as ritual funerary objects and also planted along the outside of the *kofun*. Although textbooks love to illustrate *haniwa* with the figures of horse and a soldier, the most common type of non-cylindrical *haniwa* represented a female shaman. Perhaps the terracotta-colored androgynous human *haniwa* figure in the shrinebox has journeyed from the past to pay tribute to Yamamba-chan.

Joining the mythological yamamba are photos of young women from a subset of a marginal street fashion who were derisively nicknamed yamamba.[9] Beginning in the 1990s, a new female subcultural group emerged that was tagged with the label *kogyaru* (a clipped form of *kōkōsei gyaru*, high school girl). They captured media attention not only for their appearance—short skirts, loose socks, deep tans, and bleached hair—but also for their seeming break from prescriptive norms for girls and women. Many adults thought their language and behaviors were too self-assured, too impertinent, too vulgar. *Kogyaru* who pushed the style to an extreme limit spent time in the tanning salon until they reached a maximum tan that earned them the name *ganguro* (face black). Swaths of white eyeshadow ringed their eyes, and white lipstick accentuated the deep saddle-brown of their skin. From the perspective of both *kogyaru* and *ganguro*, their fashion and behaviors served to resist both class-based beauty norms and gendered expectations. Most adults found them horrifying and incomprehensible.

Members of the subculture faced massive verbal abuse as they roamed city districts. One famous *ganguro* model named Buriteri recounted in interviews how people on the street yelled at her that she was disgusting, and some called her a cockroach. Middle-aged men accustomed to cute, docile young women were particularly repulsed by the *ganguro*. Critics writing in men's magazines began to refer to them as yamamba, alluding to the white hair and unattractive appearance of the mountain witch. In defiance, the young women adopted the intended insult and used it to affectionately refer to themselves and their friends. Eventually, the cheeky clipped form "Mamba" became a term of endearment. Like the yamamba of folklore, the Heisei period (1989–2019) yamamba has also vanished from sight. But her rebellious and resistant spirit lives on.

An Encounter in Aokigahara

David Holloway

K's interest in Aokigahara—the so-called "Suicide Forest" of
Eastern Japan—was purely personal. Burdened with suicidal
ideation since he was a teenager, K, by the dissertation stage
of his graduate studies, was more than comfortable with the
idea of taking his own life. Indeed, he had tried to do so on
multiple occasions, the most noteworthy of attempts being
the time he washed a handful of Vicodin down his throat
using a bottle of Kettle One vodka when he was twenty-three,
as well as the time he tried hanging himself from a doorknob,
his favorite Alexander McQueen scarf wrapped aggressively
about his neck, several years later. Neither attempt was met
with even a whisper of success, leading K to conclude that he
was, in effect, stuck here.

"The body wants to live," he theorized to one of his therapists
once, "even if the mind wants to die." This was not an original theory by any means, but one rooted in Cartesian mind-
body antagonism. Descartes conceptualized the relationship
between mind and body as ontologically "problematical." To
K, this was putting it lightly.

As a life-long student of Japanese studies, K well knew that classic and contemporary Japanese thinkers had consistently offered an alternative to the mind-body problematic. Embodiment is central to Japanese phenomenology:

> Both the concepts "spirit" and "body" are kinds of extremes (i.e., concepts abstracted) used as clues for understanding life. For the most part our concrete life is spent within a structure that cannot be reduced either to the spirit or the body. Hence it is wrong to see the spirit and the body as two existential principles, and to grasp reality in their intersection and separation. Rather, we should consider this unique structure as itself fundamental, and regard the spirit and the body as aspects abstracted from it.

To K, there was a certain degree of liberation, even comfort, in thinking of mind and body as parts of an epistemological whole.

Furthermore, the Japanese just *seemed* comfortable with suicide. Early in his graduate career, K did extensive ethnographic research on what drives the Japanese to take their lives with almost casual regularity. Key to his studies was a close reading of *The Complete Manual of Suicide*, or *Kanzen jisatsu manyuaru*. K reasoned that the success of such a book (it has been reprinted three times since its first printing in 1993) illuminates important dimensions of the Japanese political unconscious. In his publications on the subject, such as "The Cultural Politics of Suicide in Japan" (*World Journal of Suicide* 13.1), K drew attention to the legacy of *seppuku* on the battlefields during the middle ages, the ubiquity of suicide chat rooms in the contemporary era, and, most importantly, the lack of any moral, ethical, or religious injunctions against suicide in the Japanese social fabric.

In this context, Aokigahara, an unauthorized sanctuary for the emotionally tormented to take their own lives, simply made sense.

K made up his mind: under the guise of dissertation research, he would travel to Aokigahara. He wouldn't return. K's passion for the subject of suicide, dedication to his studies, and intellectual acumen made it relatively easy for him to receive the blessings from his Japanese studies department at X University. In addition, Aokigahara remained untouched in critical scholarship. Novels had been written about it; tabloids had published on it; and films had been made—but scholars had yet to make the forest the subject of critical inquiry. "Aokigahara," he argued in his dissertation prospectus, "reminds us of the precarity of life while underscoring the fact that life as such is shaped and reshaped by pointed cultural, social, ethnic, and spiritual mechanisms. As much as the 'Suicide Forest' can teach us about Japanese conceptions of death, then, it can also, and more importantly, teach us about Japanese views toward life."

✳

Occupying an expanse of land on the northwestern edge of Mount Fuji, formed from hardened lava when the volcano last erupted in 864 CE, Aokigahara is dense and largely impenetrable. Known colloquially, and less sensationally than its other moniker, as the "Sea of Trees," the forest provides a natural sense of quietude. Because of its density, visitors often mark their paths with string or plastic tape. Stories abound of ghosts (*yūrei*) of suicide victims roaming the grounds. Such victims number approximately one hundred per year.

K was more than familiar with the stories and legends that haunted Aokigahara. Not one to believe in much of anything, K tended to dismiss all of that as the musings of the bored. He arrived at Aokigahara after a quick taxi drive from the local station.

"Don't go in there," the elderly driver warned K. He had kind eyes and a soft voice. "Even tourists get lost and some never find their way out. Haven't you heard? It's cursed."

"I appreciate your concern," K responded in his best polite Japanese. "I know the stories. I brought lots of string," he continued with a mild smile. K felt bad lying to the driver. He had no string. In his backpack: a Hello Kitty notepad, a Montblanc pen, rope, a bottle of water, assorted snacks, a blanket, a vial of sleeping pills, a small candle, a knife, matches, and a windbreaker.

"It's especially dangerous at night," warned the driver, locking eyes with K in the rearview mirror. "But I guess everything is. So just be careful, yeah?"

"I will."

The driver pulled into a small parking lot. On the far edge of the lot was a line of schoolchildren piling into a dirty school bus. They had cameras, were fidgety and excited. It was dusk. The sun was beginning to vanish behind Mount Fuji's majesty.

"I hope you know what you're doing. Don't do anything drastic," the driver said with concern.

On the drive to Aokigahara, K had explained his research project. The driver expressed fascination but, in retrospect, probably had his doubts. Nobody who goes into the bowels of Aokigahara really has plans to come out.

✳

The path into the forest's inner clockwork was well worn. Tourists and curious sorts made Aokigahara a regular destination. And, true to rumors, there were pieces of string tied around a number of the trees that lined K's way. Some trees had ribbons, others were marked with a large "X." K thought of Hansel and Gretel's breadcrumb trail and a faint smile drifted to his lips.

The sun was mostly gone. What light that reached K was obfuscated by the forest's canopy. The air was chilly. Roots from aged trees breached the ground in places, making K's trek somewhat treacherous. The path beneath his feet grew sparse and trees marked with string, tape, and the like grew even sparser. K trudged on, purposefully weaving between trees, under branches—making sure to get good and lost. Leaves and pine needles crackled under his feet; animals and insects made noises to his left and right. K's breath ruffled in his ears.

It would be dark soon. That's when K would stop walking to begin his rites. By candlelight, he would pen a note to his mother. Then he would fashion a noose from his length of rope. He would find a sturdy branch. He would swallow his vial of sleeping pills. Finally, K would pray. To whom or what, he was unsure. But it would be an appropriate thing to do.

K walked on for a short time before settling on his location. At the base of a mighty tree, K set his pack down and unzipped it.

Then he heard something.

＊

Something shrill that cut through the murky silence. Something human. He heard it again. A woman's voice. K couldn't make out what the voice was saying; it was too far away. But it was in distress, K could tell that much. Whatever the woman was saying, she was saying it over and over again, at regular intervals—like a dusty record skipping in time.

K stopped what he was doing and twisted his head toward the noise. He was unsure, but there was a certain quality to her voice: whoever she was, she sounded old.

He gave a slight shrug. *Not my problem*. He bent back to his pack and began riffling through it. The woman continued to wail in the distance.

Help me.

K stopped what he was doing. That's what she was saying— *Help me. Help me.* The woman's voice felt, to K, sharper, clearer. And again: *Help me.* Like a thunderstorm, she was getting closer with each utterance. *Help me.* She was headed toward K.

K couldn't tell which direction the noise was coming from, but soon the woman would reach him. He took a step backward, tripping on a fallen branch. K toppled to the ground. Reaching behind him to gather his bearings, K's hand landed on what felt like a human foot. It was fleshy, cold. It felt dirty. K recoiled and hurriedly righted himself. He turned, in spite of himself, toward whatever or whoever was behind him.

Help me! She croaked through crooked, unsightly teeth. She was old. Her white hair, long and knotted, was splotched with gray. Her face was creased with wrinkles. Her eyes, clouded with cataracts. *Help me!* She spat again. She seemed not to see K; rather she looked right through him. The woman held a rotten staff. Her fingernails were warped and malnourished.

K had heard the legends—elderly women being taken to the mountains and left to die: *obasute.* He had also heard the other legends—crones inhabiting the mountains, preying on hapless individuals who wander through their wood: *yamamba.*

K was frozen with fear.

The woman extended a shaky hand, uncurled an ugly finger, and pointed at K as though marking him for death.

Lore teaches that such mountain hags are embittered and vengeful. Some eat men, others devour children. Some have terrible, teethed openings on the tops of their heads, others appear as beautiful maidens possessing the souls of hungry demons. Back at X University, K's thesis advisor was an expert on these tales.

The woman croaked again: *Help me.*

Tasukete.

She could, or at least would, say nothing else. In this light, she was paradoxically harmless. She did not appear to want to eat K; she was in pain.

The fear that had initially gripped K began to subside as he took in the visage before him. Behind the awfulness of her appearance, she was a victim. Her leathery, wrinkled skin showed signs of harm—scars, like railroad tracks, traveled the length of her arms. And her neck was marked with a faint ring, like a halo that had slipped from above her head. She was a woman whose body reflected a life of abuse and neglect. K should not have been afraid; he should have been moved. And to be sure, K was overtaken with sympathy. It dawned on him that her external scars reflected his own inner strife.

This woman, this hag, this crone; she was to be pitied. K, too, was to be pitied. A warped pair, these two individuals were broken reflections of each other.

She continued to wail. The sun had completely set, and her figure was claimed by the darkness. K fetched the candle from his pack. He also fetched his length of rope and knife. In that moment, K made a decision. He lit the candle, which provided a laughable quantity of light. Then, with his knife, he cut the length of rope in two. Then into thirds. And, finally, quarters. He fetched his vial of sleeping pills, tossed it into the night.

K stepped toward the woman, the *yamamba*. Her eyebrows quivered as her clouded eyes searched in vain for his figure. *Tasukete ...*

K thought about all the times he cried out for help—suicide attempts, depression, drug addiction. Nobody had ever been there for him. He extended an ambivalent hand toward the woman.

In that moment, in the darkness, the woman's mouth mutated into a terrible smile. She lunged at K, jagged teeth shimmering in the moonlight.

The Smile of a Mountain Witch
(*Yamamba no bishō*)

Ōba Minako, translated by Noriko Mizuta Lippit, assisted by Mariko Ochi

I would like to tell you about a legendary witch who lives in the mountains. Her straggly gray hair tied with string, she waits there for a man from the village to lose his way, meaning to devour him. When an unknowing young man asks to be put up for the night, the owner of the house grins, a comb with teeth missing here and there clutched between her teeth. As he feels a cold chill run up and down his spine beholding this eerie hag of a woman, her yellowed teeth shining under the flickering lamp, she says, "You just thought 'What an uncanny woman she is! Like an old, monster cat!' didn't you?"

Startled, the young man thinks to himself, "Don't tell me she's planning to devour me in the middle of the night!"

Stealing a glance at her from under his brows, the man gulps down a bowl of millet porridge. Without a moment's hesitation she tells him, "You just thought in your mind, 'Don't tell me she's planning to devour me in the middle of the night!' didn't you!"

The man, turning pale, quickly replies, "I was just thinking that with this warm bowl of porridge I finally feel relaxed, and that my fatigue is catching up with me." But with his body as hard as ice, he thinks to himself, "The reason she's boiling such a big pot of water must be because she is preparing to cook me in it in the middle of the night!"

With a sly grin, the old witch says, "You just thought to yourself, 'The reason she's boiling such a big pot of water must be because she is preparing to cook me in it in the middle of the night!' didn't you?"

The man becomes even more terrified. "You accuse me wrongly. I was only thinking that I'm really tired from walking all day and that I ought to excuse myself and retire for the night while I'm still warm from the porridge, so that I may start early tomorrow morning."

But he thinks to himself, "What a spooky old hag! This monster cat of a woman must be one of those old witches who live up in the mountains I hear so much about. Or else she wouldn't read my mind so well!"

Without a moment's delay, the mountain witch says, "You just thought, 'What a spooky old hag! This monster cat of a woman must be one of those old witches who live up in the mountains I hear so much about. Or else she wouldn't read my mind so well!'"

The man becomes so frightened that he can hardly keep his teeth from chattering, but he manages to shuffle his body along on his shaking knees. He says, "Well, let me excuse myself and retire ..."

Practically crawling into the next room, the man lays his body down on a straw mat without even undoing his traveling attire. The old witch follows him with a sidelong glance and says, "You're thinking to yourself now that you'll wait to find the slightest chance to escape."

Indeed, the man had lain down hoping to take her off her guard, so that he might find an opportunity to run away.

In any case, these old mountain witches are able to read a person's mind every time, and in the end the victim runs for his life away from her abode. The old witch pursues him, and the man just keeps running for his life. At least this is the form the classic mountain-witch tales assume.

But surely these old witches cannot have been wrinkled old hags from birth. At one time they must have been babies with skin like freshly pounded rice cakes and the faint, sweet-sour odor peculiar to the newborn. They must have been maidens seducing men with their moist, glossy complexions of polished silk. Their shining nails of tiny pink shells must have dug into the shoulders of men who suffocated in ecstasy between their lovers' plump breasts.

For one reason or another, however, we never hear about young witches living up in the mountains. It seems that the young ones cannot bear to remain in their hermitage, and their stories become transformed into stories of cranes, foxes, snowy herons, or other beasts or birds. They then become beautiful wives and live in human settlements.

These beasts that disguise themselves as human women invariably make extremely faithful spouses; they are very smart and full of delicate sentiments. Yet their fate somehow is inevitably tragic. Usually by the end of their tales they run back into the mountains, their fur or feathers pitifully fallen. Perhaps these poor creatures, with all their bitterness and resentment, turn into mountain witches. After all, devouring may be an expression of ultimate affection. Does not a mother in an emotional moment often squeeze her child and exclaim, "You're so dear to me I could eat you up!"?

Now, the woman about whom I am going to speak was a genuine mountain witch.

She died at the age of sixty-two.

At sixty-two, when her soulless body was cleansed with rubbing alcohol, her skin was bright and juvenescent like the wax figure of a goddess. Her hair was half-white, and on the mound at the end of her gently sloping belly were a few strands of silver. Yet around her calmly shut eyelids and her faintly smiling lips lingered a strange innocence and the bashfulness of a little girl who is forcing a smile even though she is about to burst out crying.

Indeed, she was the mountain witch of mountain witches. But even though she often longed for a hermitage on the mountains, she never lived in one, and she spent her entire life in the dwellings of a human settlement.

She had been a mountain witch ever since she could remember.

When she was still at a tender age and had not yet quite learned to use the bathroom, she would be so engrossed in play that she often had accidents. She would say to her mother who came running, "Oh you naughty girl. You've got to tell Mommy on time before it's too late. Oh dear, and today we don't have any change left for you—"

As her mother burst out laughing, she would go on, saying, "Really I'm no match for this child!—What can I say!"

At night, when her father was late coming home and her mother glanced at the clock on the wall, she would immediately say, "What in the world is he up to, coming home late night after night! He says it's work but I know he's really staying out as late as possible because it's so boring at home. As if he's the only one who feels that way!—Dear me—"

At that her mother would cast a wry grin and scowl at her. But before she could say anything, the little girl would exclaim, "You foolish girl! Come on, go to bed now. Little children who stay up late never grow, and they have to stay little for ever and ever."

The mother, utterly amazed at her daughter reading her mind time after time, would give in, saying, "This child is very bright, but she really tires me out!"

When she was a little older and her mother bought her a new toy, she would say, "This will keep her quiet for a while." Her mother, no doubt a little irritated, looked at her daughter, who would then say, "Why in the world does this child read other people's minds all the time. She's like a mountain witch. I wonder if people will come to dislike her like a mountain witch."

These are, of course, the kinds of things that her mother thought of often, and the child was merely verbalizing her mother's thoughts.

When she started going to school, the mother was, to a certain extent, relieved that she had times of separation from her daughter. But when she began to notice that her daughter ceased to read people's minds and became quieter each day, she asked, "How come you are so quiet now that you go to school?"

Her daughter replied, "When I say whatever is on my mind, people give me unpleasant looks, so I decided not to speak out any more. Grown-ups are happy when children act stupidly—as though they don't know anything. So from now on I've decided to keep grown-ups happy."

The mother responded firmly in a manner befitting one who had borne a mountain witch. "You say whatever is on your mind. You don't have to pretend. You're a child, remember?"

But the child merely regarded her mother with a disdainful smile.

All in all, the child performed well at school. On the occasions when she did not do well in a test, she would tear it up without showing it to her mother. Her mother would complain when she did not finish the lunch she brought to school, so on days when she did not have much of an appetite, she threw the remaining contents of her lunchbox into a trashcan on her way home. But so that her mother would not become suspicious, she left a little portion of it every now and then and showed it to her mother, saying, "The teacher talked longer today, so I didn't have enough time to finish it."

Time passed, and the child bloomed into maidenhood, but because her family was not well-to-do her mother could not afford to buy her expensive dresses. When the two went shopping together, the girl would purposely pick the dress her mother thought most adequate and pretended that she really liked it.

She would say instead of her mother, "I think this is really sweet. If I wore something extravagant at my age, I would give people the impression that I'm someone like the mistress of a rich old man."

On such occasions her mother would look at her with a slightly sad expression on her face. And on the way home, she would buy her daughter something way beyond her means. The girl would pretend not to notice her mother's impulse and showed a happy face to her as though she was genuinely pleased by her new acquisition.

The girl would assume whatever behavior was expected of her as though it was what came naturally to her, not only toward her family, but toward anyone by whom she wanted to be liked. When they wanted her to laugh, she read their minds and laughed. When they wanted her not to say anything, she remained silent. When talkativeness was desired, she chatted merrily. Toward a person who considered himself intelligent, she would act a little stupid—she did not overdo this, for usually this type of person thought it a waste of time to deal with stupid people—and as for those who were stupid, she appreciated their simplicity.

Perhaps because she demanded too much of herself and because she wanted too many people to like her, she had to spend an incredible amount of mental energy every day. So that before she realized it she had become antisocial, reading books in her room all day, avoiding being with others.

When her mother asked, "Why don't you go out with your friends?" she would answer with few words, "Because I get tired—"

The mother, too, began to feel fatigued when she was with her daughter. When she was not around her, she felt relieved. She began to long for the day when her daughter would find an adequate young man and leave her. In other words, the mother and daughter came to the natural phase of life when they would part from each other.

The daughter, too, knew that she was a burden to her mother—in fact, she had sensed that she was a burden to her as far back as she could remember—and she wanted to free her mother, as well as herself. At the same time, somewhere in her heart she held a grudge against her mother, a grudge which was sometimes so strong that she would feel surges of inexplicable rage. That is to say, she was going through the short, rebellious phase of puberty, but when she realized that her hatred and anger were directed at the cunning ways of her mother who had become her competitor of the same sex—that is, at her dishonest ways like taking advantage of her authority as a mother and avoiding direct competition—she became acutely aware that her mother had aged and that she herself had matured.

As a mature girl, she naturally came to know a man. He was an ordinary, run-of-the-mill type of man. Typical for one who had been doted on by his mother, he firmly believed that because his mother was of the opposite sex, he was allowed beyond all reason to express himself as freely as he pleased. When one such as he matures physically, the woman he marries has to be a substitute for his mother. For him, she has to be as magnanimous as a mother, as dignified as a goddess. She has to love him limitlessly and blindly like an idiot, yet at the same time have a spirit capable of being possessed by evil, like that of some sinister beast. Fortunately, however, he at least had the male characteristic of liking women.

Since the woman was gratified by the man, she came to think that she would not mind making all kinds of efforts to keep him happy. But this turned out to be very hard labor, for after all, every corner of his mind was transparent to her. If only one could not see another's heart one would not become weary and would be able to live happily.

First of all, the man wanted the woman to be constantly jealous, so that she had to make every effort to appear that way. When another woman's shadow approached the man's life, she would act as though her presence made her competitive, and the man would be satisfied.

"Please don't go away from me. I can't live without you, you know that. I can't do anything by myself and I'm helpless when you're gone," she would cry as she sobbed and clung to him. And as she said the words, she would have the illusion that she really was a weak and incompetent creature.

Also, the man desired the woman to think of other men as something less than what they were, so that she had to close her eyes to the merits of other men and observe only their vices. But since the man was not excessively stupid, he did not allow her to denigrate others with idle speculation either. To please him, she had to make the right judgments, as well as be aware of all their vices, and indicate that even though they might have certain merits, these merits were certainly not to her liking. Thus every little opinion she expressed had to be well thought out.

On top of that, the man had the strange tendency of feeling pleasure in possessing all to himself a woman who was constantly being pursued by other men. Thus he tended to encourage rather than endure her affected flirtations. Perhaps deep down, all men long to become a part of the species of men we term "pimps."

To provide all the examples of this kind would take forever. In any case, at times the woman would forget to be jealous, or to flirt with other men. Or occasionally she was careless enough to express her true feelings about attractive men. At such times the man would become bored and think the woman lazy, thick-skinned, and lacking in sensitivity. Moreover, even when the woman succeeded in behaving perfectly to his liking, he would assert with the dignified tone of a sage who knew everything, "Women are utterly unmanageable creatures, so full of jealousy, capable of only shallow ideas and small lies. They are really just timid and stupid. In English, the word man refers also to human beings, but I guess women are only capable of being human by adhering to men."

Thanks to this irrational declaration of inequality, the two managed to live somewhat happily. Both the man and the woman grew old, and soon enough the man reached the age at which he would grumble all year long about something being wrong in this part of his body or that. He demanded that the woman worry about him all of the time and said that if anything happened to him he would be so concerned about her who would be left behind, that he would not die in peace. As she acted nervous and uneasy about him, she really became nervous and uneasy, until eventually she came to feel that he really was critically ill. For after all, unless she believed it he would not be at peace, and unless he were at peace, she could not feel that way either. Thus even though she hated nursing to such a degree that she thought she would die if she had to commit herself to it, she became a nurse just as a woman driven into a corner might sell her chastity. Observing the woman who now took up nursing, the man commended her, saying that nursing was an occupation truly in keeping with her instincts, and that as far as nursing was concerned, women were blessed with God-given talents against which no man could compete.

Around that time, the woman became exceedingly fat, so much so that when she walked just a little her shoulders would heave with every breath just like those of a pregnant woman. The main reason for this was that she was the possessor of exceptionally healthy digestive organs and consequently was constantly plagued by enormous appetites. But on top of that, she had the pitiful characteristic of wanting to make others feel good; even if she did not like it, she would eat up whatever was offered to her in order not to disappoint the person. Since other people thought that she just loved to eat, they would be terribly offended should she refuse the food that they offered her. On the other hand, her husband often boasted that he was a man of iron will. As she ate, saying, "Oh dear, here I go again—" he would cast a ridiculing glance at her; "You're such a weak-willed woman—" Even if someone put her heart into cooking something to please him, he would adamantly refuse if it was something that was not good for his health. In other words, his nerves were tenacious enough not to register shame at ignoring somebody else's feelings.

Because his use of words such as strength of will, insensitivity, and laziness so differed from hers, she would at times be overwhelmed by a sense of acute loneliness. She would come to fear not only her husband but many of the others around her as well, feeling as though she were surrounded by foreigners who did not speak the same language. Sometimes she thought she would rather live as a hermit in the depths of the mountains, just as she locked herself up in her room all day without playing when she was a little girl.

Far off in the midst of the mountains there would be nobody to trouble her, and she would be free to think as she pleased. The thought of extorting all those who tormented her in the human world made her heart beat with excitement: all those dull-headed, slow-witted people who could walk around with the looks of smug, happy heroes just because they were not capable of reading other people's hearts. If only she could say out loud like the legendary witches, "You just thought—didn't you!" how relieved she would feel! It would be the sensation of slitting the skin around the temples in order to let horns grow, horns which are itching to grow out but cannot.

When she imagined herself living alone in the mountains, she likened herself to a beautiful fairy, sprawled in the fields, naked under the benevolent sun, surrounded by trees and grasses and animals. But once a familiar human being appeared from the settlement, her face would change into that of an ogress. He would stare at her, mouth open like an idiot, and utter coarse, incoherent, conceited words, making her fly into a rage.

On such occasions, her husband would appear, dressed shabbily like a beggar. He would wander about the abode of the woman who had now changed her appearance, and like a mischievous boy who had lost a fight he would mumble, "Without her to camouflage my unreasonable desires for me, I'd be done for—"

Listening to his voice, she would look at her face reflected in a clear spring. Then she would see that half her face was smiling like an affectionate mother, while the other half was seething with demonic rage. Blood would trickle down from half her mouth while it devoured and ripped the man's flesh apart. The other half of her lips was caressing the man who curled up his body in the shadow of one of her breasts, sucking it like a baby.

Now, as she became fatter, she began to develop arteriosclerosis, for her veins were put under increasing pressure. She found numbness in various joints of her body and suffered from headaches and the sound of ringing in her ears. When she saw a physician, he diagnosed that she was merely going through menopause. She was told in her early forties that she was suffering from menopause, and since then for over twenty years she had continued to receive the same explanation.

The man asserted that women were, as a rule, more durably constructed than men, their bodies and souls being more sturdily built. He pointed to a statistic that showed how women outlive men, and insisted that between the two of them, he would be the first to go. The woman thought that perhaps the reason women live longer has something to do with the fact that men end their lives of their own accord at youth, owing to war and other violent behavior, but since it was bothersome for her to prove this statistically, she just did not bring it up.

"That's right. Even though men are larger in build, they are actually sensitive at heart and more frail. That's why all women like men." As she said this, she told herself that the world would be a place of darkness without men, even though what she said was altogether fictitious, and continued stroking the man who complained that it hurt him here or there. In order to cook and feed him food as delicate as a little bird's, she spent hours day after day.

She knew that her own fat body did not have long to last with hardened arteries, but she could think of no other way to live than to provide food for the little bird of a man who believed that he was frail.

One morning, she examined herself thoroughly in the mirror. Her face was covered with wrinkles, giving her the appearance of a mountain witch. Her yellowed teeth were uneven and ugly like those of an aged cat. White frost had fallen on her hair and she felt chilling pain as though frost columns were noisily springing up all over her body.

She felt a slight numbness as though her body belonged

to someone else. It was a stiffness related to the vague memory of her mother, long gone, far away. Somewhere, her flowing blood ebbed, and she felt dizzy. Suddenly a slight drowsiness attacked her, and when she came to herself her limbs were paralyzed and her consciousness dimmed as she felt various parts of her body gradually grow colder.

Customarily, she would have been up a long time ago preparing his meal. But finding her instead next to himself (they had slept alongside each other for forty years) face down and as stiff as a dead person, he became alarmed, and immediately straightening his body about which he had been complaining so much, he carried his wife to the hospital. Surprisingly enough, the physician who up until the day before had written her off as a case of menopause, now declared as if he were another man that she had the symptoms of cerebral thrombosis, and that if luck was against her she would only survive the next day or two. The man became totally confused, but he managed to pull himself together and decided that the first thing he should do was to send for their son and daughter, both of whom lived far away. The two children came immediately and with their father crouched around their mother who had now lost her speech.

Probably the next two days were the best two days of her life. The three of them took turns rubbing her arms and legs, and they would not leave it to the nurse to take care of even her most basic needs.

Even after two days, however, there was no drastic deterioration in their mother's condition; nor did it take a turn for the better. Her consciousness, however, became even dimmer, and she could no longer recognize the people around her. The uncertain physician said, "Considering her weight, her heart

is strong. She may be able to hold on longer than expected."
Soon the son claimed that he could not continue to stay away
from work and that since it looked as though there would be
no changes in the immediate future, he would return home
for a while. With a gloomy look on her face, the daughter
began to worry about her husband and children.

The poor man became anxious that he would not know
what to do if his daughter left, so he pleaded with her to stay
on. He sounded so helpless that the daughter, as worried as
she was about her own family, reluctantly agreed to remain.

The daughter remembered the time when she had been
critically ill as a child. Then her mother had stayed up for
days watching over her. She thought that if not for this woman
who lay in front of her unconscious, straying between life and
death, she would not have been alive today. And this might be
the last time she would be able to see her. Thinking through
these matters, she hung on beside her. But when another two
days passed, she began to wonder how long her mother would
remain in her present condition, unable to converse and barely
breathing, like a living corpse. She even thought that although
the sixty-two years her mother had lived might be shorter than
average, sooner or later everyone has to die, and that perhaps
even if her mother went as she was from her present state, she
would be considered fortunate that she could go watched over
by her husband and daughter.

The daughter felt strangely uneasy when she remembered
the story of the patient who survived for two years on intrave-
nous feeding. She became worried whether her father's savings
would be sufficient to pay the medical expenses should her
mother survive as long. Even aside from the expenses, moreover, she thought that neither she nor her brother could afford

to take care of her mother for such a long period of time, for they had their own families to consider.

She happened to think of her five-year-old daughter whom she had left behind with her mother-in-law. She remembered that at that age she herself had fallen ill and run a high fever for days, nearly contracting meningitis. Vividly, she envisioned her mother becoming frantic with worrying by her bedside, cowering over her in their house which had become pitifully unkempt. Odd as it may seem, the impact of this memory led her thoughts away from her dying mother who lay moaning between life and death in front of her eyes, and made her concerned with the possibility of her own daughter falling ill while she was away. Unlikely as it may seem, she became plagued with fear at the thought of it.

Unaware of her daughter's worries, the mother survived another two days, occasionally staring into space with empty eyes and moaning something incomprehensible. The daughter woke up the third morning, too weary to climb out of bed after a week of intensive nursing. It was a dull, gloomy morning, typical of a cloudy day in the cherry season. She looked vacantly at the profile of her unconscious mother, who was also breathing quietly and who, with hollower cheeks, looked younger and beautiful.

When the morning round was over, the daughter, remembering that her mother's body was dirty, asked the physician if she could wash the patient. He instructed the nurse to do it and left the room. Soon the nurse came back, and in a very businesslike manner, carried out her duties as instructed, turning the patient over as though she were a log.

Timidly, the daughter helped her. Just when the patient was rolled over, stripped of her nightclothes soiled with perspiration and excrement, her eyes suddenly opened wide, staring at her daughter who happened to be standing right in front of her, holding her. She smiled faintly at her as light returned to her eyes. The radiance was like that of a firecracker, bright yet sad and ephemeral. Soon the firecracker died. The invalid lost the light in her eyes, and the saliva which had gathered trickled down the side of her mouth. Her throat went into a momentary spasm. The pupils of her eyes stopped moving, and then she was still. It all happened in a single moment.

At this sudden change, the nurse hurried off to call the physician. He rushed in and started to perform artificial respiration. He also injected cardiac medication through a thick needle into her heart. It looked more like shaking an animal that had failed in the middle of an experiment than dealing with a living human being. But in any case, it is certain that the people around her made various efforts to revive the pulse to her heart which had stopped.

The woman died.

No, it would be more truthful to say that she summoned up the last of her strength to suffocate her own self and body by washing down the accumulated saliva into her windpipe.

In the last smile she exchanged with her daughter, she clearly read her daughter's mind. Her daughter's eyes said to her that she did not want to be tied down by her any longer. "Mother, I don't need you to protect me anymore. You've outlived your usefulness. If you have to be dependent on me, if you can't take care of yourself without being a burden to others, please, mother, please disappear quietly. Please don't torment me any longer. I, too, am preparing myself so that I won't trouble my daughter as I am being troubled by you. I'm willing to go easily. That's right. I ought to go easily.

I never want to be the kind of parent who, just because she doesn't have the courage to come to terms with that resolution, continues to press her unwanted kindnesses upon her offspring." It seemed that her daughter, the product of her and her husband, possessed a strength of will that was twofold. Either she would overcome all temptation, exercise moderation, and live sturdily until the moment of her death at a hundred, or live haughtily and selfishly to the end, retaining the energy to kill herself at eighty. In either case, the woman was satisfied with the daughter she had borne and raised.

Through her daughter's face, she saw the son who was not there, walking among the crowds of the metropolis. He was talking to her with a crooked smile on his face. "Mother, I have incessantly chirping chicks at home. I myself don't know why I have to keep on putting food in their mouths. But when I catch myself, I'm always flying toward my nest, carrying food in my beak. Before I even think about it, I'm doing it. If I were to stop carrying food to them and stay close by you all the time, the human race would have perished a long time ago. In other words, for me to do as I do for them is the only way in which I can prolong and keep the blood you gave me—"

Next she looked at her husband, who was standing around absentmindedly. This deranged old man, his head drooping, was touched by the beauty of his wife's naked body and absorbed self-righteously in the faithfulness that let him attend to his wife until the very end. The greatest happiness for a human being is to make another happy. She was satisfied with this man who had the capability to turn any situation into happiness, and she blessed the start of the second chapter of his life. At the same time, she thought she heard the pealing of her funeral bells.

With her own hands, she arranged her white shroud, left side under the right. In a dry riverbed, when she happened to look behind her, she saw somebody running away with his hair disheveled in the rushing wind. When she asked another deceased traveler whom she had not noticed before, the traveler answered, "He's being chased by a mountain witch."

Under the shroud which she had arranged, she felt the heartbeat of a mountain witch reviving, and she smiled. The heart of the mountain witch was throbbing as sturdily as ever. Only the blood vessels to transmit her vitality were closed, tightly, harshly, never to open again.

The time had come for the spirit of the mountain witch to return to the quiet mountains. The day had at last arrived when she would stand on a mountain ledge, her white hair swaying in the raging wind, sounding her eternal roar into the mountains. The transient dream of living in the human settlement disguised as an animal was now over.

The days she spent dreaming of living alone in the mountains, the sorrow she felt as a little girl when she first began to dislike humans, all came back to her and she shook her head. Had she lived up in the mountains, she would have been the mountain witch who devours humans from the settlement.

She wondered which would be the happier, to live in the mountains and become a man-eating witch, or to have the heart of a mountain witch and live in the settlement. But now she knew that either way it would not have made much difference. If she had lived in the mountains, she would have been called a mountain witch. Living in the settlement she could have been thought of as a fox incarnate or an ordinary woman with a sturdy mind and body who lived out her natural life.

That was the only difference, and either way it would have been all the same.

Just before she took her last breath, it crossed her mind that her own mother must have been a genuine mountain witch as well. Strangely enough, when she died she had a mysteriously naive face with the innocent smile of a newborn baby. Sobbing and clinging to this woman who died in peace, the daughter, with swollen eyes which told of her indescribable relief, said, "Such a beautiful death mask—Mother, you really must have been a happy woman." Her husband cried silently with wide open eyes full of tears like a fish.

Yamamba's Laughter and Other Poems: An Introduction

*Mizuta Noriko, translated by Rebecca Copeland and Marianne Tarcov**

The yamamba has been a constant companion to compara-tive literature scholar and poet Mizuta Noriko. Her fascina-tion emerged in the early 1980s with her translation of Ōba Minako's short story "The Smile of a Mountain Witch" and was amplified in her 1995 dialogue with Ōba on the yamamba in Japanese culture. Mizuta has contributed to our under-standing of the yamamba through her many published trans-lations and essays but also in her poetry. Originally written in Japanese, the ten poems collected here are translated into English by Japanese-literature scholars Rebecca Cope-land (the first three) and Marianne Tarcov (the following seven). As with any work of translation, these come with challenges. The evocative suggestiveness of Mizuta's poetic language is easily marred by a translation that is too precise. And yet English—even at its most poetic—generally prefers

---

* Material for this introduction is derived from an email between Rebecca Copeland and Mizuta Noriko (April 17, 2020) and from Mizuta's "Yamam-ba no yume: Joron to shite" in *Mizuta Noriko shishū* (Tokyo: Shichōsha, 2016): 108–23.

adherence to grammatical conventions. These demands are particularly fraught when translating from a language like Japanese that survives without precise subjects. Verbs are free to act, to speak, to move without a named protagonist. This indistinctness is essential to Mizuta. Her poems celebrate the yamamba, but they do not necessarily speak in her voice. As Mizuta explains, "I prefer leaving the subject ambiguous, impersonal, or even in the passive mode as if someone or something else, like nature, has taken the actions." For Mizuta, the yamamba is not contained in a single identity or persona. She sees her poems, rather, as a "series of prayers for, or homage to Yamamba" by those whose lived experiences have overlapped hers somewhere along the way, those who have stepped beyond the confines of "the village" (or *sato*) to make their rounds of the mountains.

As the poet explains, key to understanding the yamamba is appreciating all that is represented in "village" and "mountain." The former stands for the patriarchal family system with its chauvinistic codes of conduct and the self-denying demands placed on the women contained within. Those who cannot abide the demands of the village are forced into the mountains, either leaving of their own accord or being chased out by the village gatekeepers. Mountains stand for freedom and self-expression, but also isolation and otherness. For the sensitive village woman, for the perceptive poet, the yamamba becomes both a pitiable figure and a longed-for destination. As Mizuta Noriko's poems unfurl, the yamamba grows beyond the limiting vision of witch or hag and merges into nature itself: untamed, unnamed, unimagined.

—*Rebecca Copeland*

Yamamba of the Sato

MORNING CHORES

I toss the left-over bread into the garden.
Sparrows swoop down,
mountain pigeons sing.
This year, too, they are building nests in the garden.
The zelkova tree not yet full height.
The fern-pine hedge still without new leaves.
Has the cat come yet;
has the snake slipped in?
Eat quickly, my friends,
tedious housework awaits.
Conversations   Conversations
At the end of morning chores
I fetch water for O-Jizō-san.
The pail
cannot contain the face
of the woman
hungry
wild
her aim set—
any minute now—
just tear it off with your teeth.
That and this,
here and there
scatter it in the air.
The empty husk

gone to ash.
She returns to the mountain
to awaken the wind.

RENASCENCE

Who enclosed
this land?
The occupants thwart the ivy's spread
and chase the lithe moving mice
that burrow in from everywhere.
They poke at
the snake coiling inside the kitchen drawers
and spray poison on the wildflowers,
the black widow,
and the hornet.
This is a job for a specialist.
Such a small plot of land.
A child's shoe,
two cars and a bicycle,
the carpenter's chisel,
a glittering pole where laundry hangs,
a flowerbed for large roses,
proof of human hands.
At least in this enclosure,
this land just for us,
renascence loosens
the fear of dreams.
The skeleton
cannot stop

Laughter
rambles on
Freedom,
a discordant
dance.

YAMAMBA'S DREAM
—In the Garden 2—

Birdsong
filters into the enclosed garden
and butterflies flit between the blooms.
I hum the line
from that poet of old
"All's right with the world."

Higher than the high fence
the foliage of the striped ash.
The climbing rose
conceals the gaps in the hedge,
my tiny paradise.
Shall I take a nap?
No one
will push their way through the thorns to enter.

Swept clean   light pours
A safe place.
In the corner the covered well.
I've finally fought my way here.
Walking along the bank of the waterless river.
Secretly watching for   the landmark;
tossing aside shredded memories.

Neither assassin nor prince will enter
my miniature universe.
I am sovereign of this tiny space.
The sound of the distant water does not reach my ears.

I rule
this moment of eternal afternoon.

> Exposing the burn scars on her arm
> the woman naps,
> living on the riverside, staring down the enemy
> children,
> she follows the feathered robe.
> Camped in a tent on the beach,
> she eats snakes to stave off hunger.
> The sound inside her ears
> harmonizes with the wind in the skies,
> circles round the mountain ridges that protrude
> from the dream tableau.
> Now   the unbound body of the massive woman
> stretches
> right atop the timeline   like the horizon at dusk
> forever

The crows peck apart memories
dry as the well.
When I awaken from my nap,
shall I clean the garden again?
Today,
I can't expect a sunset.
I'll close the gate early.

Translated by Rebecca Copeland

"Yamamba no yume" originally appeared in *Mizuta Noriko shishū* (Tokyo: Shichōsha, 2016): 65–66.

Yamamba of the Mountains

Mountains stretch on.
Sunken into the sea,
pushed up into the highest peak
the gentle slope of undeveloped land,
a city's hill
forever
limitlessly stretching on,
bearing
the things that mount it.
In the wind
the yamamba drowses
her body moving invisibly
Its trembling
passes
settles
pierces
time's
waves
So this is a dream
her unawakened consciousness,
wordless
soul
entrusted to the mountains
makes the rounds

She birthed them
like oleaster seeds
one   after another
And fed them
their whole bodies swelling,
vomiting.
She nursed them
brimming with falling pomegranate seeds
gathering them one by one
wiping away the oozing liquid
sheltering them in her palm.

Abandoned memories
in the alder's shade
Waves of mountains, layer upon layers
Left-over dreams
Picking through pebbles

She birthed them
one   after another
She fed them
breath by breath
She nursed them
Until her breasts wrinkled,
one   by one.

Within the torn wing
A hollow left by eaten grass
The repair of the birthing hut
can wait until tomorrow

YAMAMBA'S SILENCE 2

She left
home
crossed
the border
and walked
mountain after mountain
of linked dreams
strode over and over   the dateline

She ran
like the falcon
like the wildcat
like speed itself
She ate
like a coyote
consuming
like a deer
tearing, chewing
like a cow
lying stretched
She ruminated
and slept
curling her body into a small shrine
entrusting her limbs to the earth
her hair a dwelling place for insects
braided with slim fungi
A birthing bed
for humus
for all things.

YAMAMBA'S LITANY

Hunger

deep in the grove
something makes itself felt
Turn around
and there's a shadow
dragging its long tail
and the shadow's shadow stretching and shrinking
walks in daylight
searching for food
facing the setting sun
stretching on and on and on endlessly.
Shadow
you who have no body
are you hungry?
What are you looking for?
What do you seek
following me?
The shadow's greedy hunger
eats
my footprints
conceals
my body
with a flat emptiness
my regret
my hunger.

YAMAMBA'S LAUGHTER

Gathered yesterday
chestnuts
acorns   walnuts
They laughed
The fruits of the trees all laughed
The fruits of the berry plants grabbed this morning
blueberries, silverberries, mulberries, raspberries
laughed
The berries all laugh
The mushrooms picked in the afternoon:
himeji, hatsu-dake, hen-of-the-woods,
entice with a sour smile.
The *kinoko* are all silent.
The tree bark torn off in the evening
the bent and broken twigs
laugh loudly
burning
blazing
smoking
until they become ash.
In loud voices
they laugh and laugh,
these small things

Tempted,
the mountains
are laughing

DEATH OF A MOUNTAIN PERSON

On the next mountain
someone died
In the sack the person carried was a single bamboo flute
Come to think of it,
like the distant howling of wolves,
the wild breath of running beasts,
the rustle of evening trees,
the cries
of birds' dreams,
awake as the dead of night ends
to find a package
a sack,
a swelling sack
Inside
an unpleasantly cool
damp-earth smell.
The sack enters the body
Inside the body
is a single bamboo flute.
This dream
is a bad dream.
Wolves' hunger
The sound they make tearing the sack apart
trying to break through
like thunder.
This dream
is a good dream.
The chirping birds
prepare to wake

From far away
it comes
surging
covering
satisfied.
In the waves
sleeping two thousand years
In one more year it will be remembered
when the bamboo flute
awakes

YAMAMBA'S SILENCE 3

Sleeping Yamamba

Bodies in a row
sleeping giants
women who read
dreams
women who draw
silence
women
who try to grasp
their limbs
with a grip so strong
it does not stop time
sightlines
unobscured by mist
The women
who try to return

the sleeping yamamba's
transforming
uncanny gaze
The watching woman dozes too
Her breath
Not erased by the wind
The listening woman naps
All
their bellies   swell
their bodies relax,
the sleeping big women
beckon
beyond the mountains
the women who do not sleep,
the women who wake

Translated by Marianne Tarcov

Dancing the Yamamba:
With Yokoshi Yasuko

Rebecca Copeland

On December 12, 2019, Rebecca Copeland conducted a "virtual interview" with choreographer Yokoshi Yasuko on the creation of her new performance production, shuffleyamamba. Rebecca was in North Carolina, the United States, and Yasuko in Kyoto, Japan. They communicated via email. Rebecca sent Yasuko a set of questions concerning her creative process, the way that it connected with the figure of the yamamba, and how Yasuko derived inspiration from earlier dance traditions. Yasuko responded, and the two continued with a "conversation" that covered a free-range of topics related to Yasuko's dance and creative imagination.

REBECCA: I had the pleasure of seeing the performance of your contemporary dance, *shuffleyamamba*, at the Eirakukan Theatre in Izushi City last October. The production left me spellbound! I especially enjoyed the way you incorporated contemporary dance, ballet, and traditional Japanese movement along with creative references to Japanese performance histories and legends. Also, the combination on stage of multimedia such as video, spoken monologue, and Gelsey

Bell's creative soundscapes felt very fresh, especially in the venerable space of the Eirakukan.

YASUKO: The choice of the theater was very important to me. In 2015, when I was working on the production of my dance "ZERO ONE" at the Kinosaki International Art Center (KIAC), I came across a leaflet for the theater in the KIAC lobby. I was immediately attracted to the beautiful architectural style of the space. It used to be a Kabuki theater, you know. But once Kabuki lost popularity, the theater saw other kinds of productions come and go: modern plays, then films, and finally it was forced to close in 1964 and stayed closed for over forty years until it was lovingly restored and reopened to the public in 2008.

Have you seen Ozu Yasujirō's film *Ukigusa* [Floating Weeds, 1958]? The film features a traveling theater troupe that goes to a small town to perform. The theater where they perform reminds me of the Eirakukan. I love the atmosphere in the theater. I love the way you feel like you're stepping back into time when you're there. You can sense the sweat and effort of past performers in the soft, lustrous floorboards of the stage.

REBECCA: It's a beautiful space. I think it took me about three or four hours to get there from Kyoto using a tricky combination of trains and buses. I was amused by the fact that in the old days, the itinerant actors would travel to the theater. But now, it's mostly the audience that does the traveling! And of course, your work, *shuffleyamamba*, is also about travel, both literal and metaphorical. I understand that your piece is based loosely on the Noh play *Yamamba*. What was it about the play that attracted you?

AYUMI TAMAKI

Yokoshi Yasuko in a promotional photograph from her 2003 solo, experimental piece "Shuffle." (Artist's New York City apartment, 2002.)

YASUKO: Initially, I was drawn to Zeami's *Yamamba* because it is about performance: an encounter between an itinerant dancer and the yamamba.

REBECCA: You mean the encounter in the play between the young dancer, Hyakuma Yamamba, and the mountain crone?

YASUKO: Right, the play concerns two women: One is young and beautiful. The other old and ugly. Already, that's an interesting encounter. But the young one emulates the old one who was once a famous dancer. Years ago she had been celebrated in the city, but now she lives deep in the mountains. The young dancer makes her living by singing and dancing about the older Yamamba, who is, in fact, a real yamamba.

These two women meet in the mountains one day. The setup for the narrative is dramatic and majestic. The massive presence of the yamamba represents an incarnation of the universal wisdom of humans, nature, and the universe.

REBECCA: The encounter between the artifice of the dancer and the true nature of the yamamba seems to suggest the Buddhist principle of non-duality, asking us to question why we must see one as true and the other as false.

YASUKO: Yes. And for me, what was most attractive about the play *Yamamba* was the fact that it is woman-centered. Unlike most Noh plays, the main characters presented on the stage are women. Most classic works throughout the world emphasize the femininity of a character by placing her in contexts that explore her relationship to a man. Usually, the focus is on the tragic connection between the woman and her lover, her husband, or her son. But in *Yamamba* the women relate to each other. It is a very special work because this female-centric viewpoint holds the center of things. That's what my co-producer Gelsey Bell and I saw.

REBECCA: Tell me about the title of your dance. *Yamamba* is recognizable from the association with the Noh play, as you've just described. But what about "shuffle"?

YASUKO: "Shuffle" is the title of my experimental solo work of contemporary dance, which I performed in New York in 2003; *shuffleyamamba* is the outcome of the creative merger between the earlier work and the way I encountered *Yamamba*.

REBECCA: I understand that in your earlier dance "Shuffle" you created a shaman-like character derived from the *Kojiki* (Record of Ancient Matters, 712) and the depiction of Japanese foundational myths. How did an ancient goddess like Izanami find her way into a contemporary dance piece?

YASUKO: It was rather unexpected. I was living in New York in 2001 and came across a translation of the *Kojiki* into English. I was strongly attracted to the story of Izanami and Izanagi as the origins of the universe. And I decided to channel Izanami into my solo dance. In the myth, Izanami—who has died and is in the underworld—continues to communicate with her husband, Izanagi.

I came up with the idea of shuffling on the stage between the story of Izanami in her world of death, known as Yomi in the myth, and the world of my mother's family, who were almost all completely lost in a shipwreck on the Seto Inland Sea in Hiroshima.

After I became an adult I began to think more and more about that legacy. It occurred to me that I had been born into this world by the death of my family. When I came across a photograph of my grandfather and uncle who perished in the wreck, I suddenly wanted to channel them onstage through my performance.

REBECCA: And so you wanted to bring that shamanic quality into "Shuffle"?

YASUKO: Yes. Ever since I was young I've felt close to these spirits. Before ballet recitals I used to call on my dead grandmother just before going on stage. I still do the same now.

Sadly, I had just begun working on "Shuffle" when New York experienced the terrorist attacks of 9/11. I watched the two towers of the World Trade Center collapse and so many lives lost, I began to think daily about the boundary between life and death.

REBECCA: In *shuffleyamamba* we can sense a similar shamanic quality and the presence of spirits. For me, seeing the way you projected the video footage of your 2003 dance "Shuffle" on the stage at different intervals made it seem like the spirit of your former dance was there. There you were (or I should say, there Izanami was)—from 2003—in the background observing the dancers in 2019. Kind of like the yamamba watching over the itinerant dancer in the Noh play. I thought it was very powerful.

YASUKO: Thank you.

REBECCA: How do you see the two dances fitting together? I mean, "Shuffle" and *shuffleyamamba*? Is Izanami a yamamba?

YASUKO: Well, the character Izanami was an iconographic female goddess just like Yamamba. And there are some scholars who believe that she is the original yamamba.

REBECCA: Once she died, she merges with nature.

YASUKO: Exactly. In *shuffleyamamba* I am also interested in the intersection between gender and creativity and the position of the body in society. Having lived in New York for thirty-five years as an immigrant, I came to understand that the body itself is political. Reading the body is also reading society and politics. And I think that reading the body is the fastest track to thinking about gender. It's complex and unanswerable, and I'm interested in something that can only be told through dance, not spoken theater. Talking in dance sounds contradictory, but stories told by the body are more dramatic and direct than stories told by words.

REBECCA: I understand that in "Shuffle" your work was controversial because of nudity and the simulation of masturbation.

YASUKO: I also walked around with a huge strap-on penis on stage which invited considerable controversy at the time in the New York dance world. That surprised me.

REBECCA: *shuffleyamamba* also includes nudity and masturbation.

YASUKO: But no penises. [Haha!]

REBECCA: No. [Laughter.] In the dance you present a kind of history of Western dance in Japan. But you also account for the importance of itinerant female performers, too, the *shirabyōshi, miko, kugutsume,* and such. These women were associated with the court or with religious institutions. But they were still regarded as marginal or promiscuous because of their public visibility, right? Their bodies were exposed to the male gaze.

YASUKO: In both Western and Japanese dance the body is an abstract object. Regardless of the function of the dance, the

The yamamba (performed by Fukuoka Sawami) is to the right, with the narrator (Ueno Narumi) to the left. A film of Izanami from "Shuffle" (performed by Yokoshi Yasuko) plays in the background.

dancer's body—by being exposed to men's eyes—is an object of display. But then on the historical Noh stage, you had men performing the roles of women. The gendering of the dancer is complicated.

REBECCA: I liked the way you created a tableau on stage during the performance of *shuffleyamamba* that seemed to suggest the lineage of dance, or at least the way the legacy of dance is passed historically from one body to another.

YASUKO: Japanese traditional arts focus on the *kata*. The *kata* is passed down from master dancer to *deshi*, or student. In order to explore the truth within the *kata*, the performer is taught to deny the self.

Western dance also has a wide variety of forms and styles, but the dancer's perspective is always the subject. The dance is "with" the body, so the self is in charge of the body. Japanese art training begins with emptying the body of the self. I think the way dancers perceive their bodies is fundamentally different in Japan and the West.

REBECCA: And in *shuffleyamamba* you make reference to the importance of this tradition of learning. In a way, your work pays homage to the many itinerant performers of the past.

YASUKO: In fact, the origin of Japanese dance, the relationship between sex and performing arts is inseparable. We see this in Kabuki, Noh, and in the earlier dances as well. In many of these traditional arts, the subject of the performance concerns female protagonists like the *shirabyōshi*, that you mentioned earlier, or maiko, geisha, or high-ranking courtesan [*oiran*, *tayū*, or *keisei*]. Much earlier in the history, a shrine maiden [*miko*], the prototype of the Japanese female performer, goes around the mountains and sells her arts but is also associated with prostitution.

From a different perspective, there's something transgressive and anti-social in the performing arts and the way performers achieve power and independence through their bodies.

REBECCA: The yamamba was also the result of transgression surely! A lone woman in the mountains! A woman believed by some to eat human flesh and prey on men!

YASUKO: The yamamba in the Noh play is not as frightening as she is powerful and majestic. The play presents the metaphor of the passing of knowledge, wisdom, and artistry among the female performance artists. *shuffleyamamba* traces this metaphor through contemporary dancers.

REBECCA: Thank you for taking time for this interview. And thank you also for creating such a richly layered work. It is complex, but that makes it so exciting. I feel like it's the kind of work that will linger and will continue to provoke ideas and questions.

YASUKO: People say my works are difficult to understand. But, I like the method of building a work by mixing my personal history with historical facts and folk tales. By delicately incorporating the "unspoken story" of the past from a very personal perspective, it transforms into a universal story of the present and the future, creating a meaningful transformation that can be experienced on the stage. The reason I make works that are said to be difficult to understand is because I want to make something that I don't understand. But when I'm making it, I think about various things and live everyday with my work.

YOKOSHI YASUKO'S choreography entwines culture and personal insights to create radical performances through the melding of dance, video, and storytelling as layered contemporary performance projects. Yokoshi was awarded a John Simon Guggenheim Memorial Foundation Fellowship (2009); she was the inaugural Resident Commissioned Artist at New York Live Arts (2011–13) and a Resident Artist at Baryshnikov Arts Center (2013). Prior to her 2008 Grants to Artists award, Yokoshi received a Creative Capital Grant (2002), two New York Dance and Performance "Bessie" Awards for her choreography of "Shuffle" (2003) and "what we when we" (2006), and a BAXten Award (2007). Yokoshi earned a B.A. in Choreography from Hampshire College in 1986. She currently resides in Kyoto, Japan.

Glossary

bodhisattva (Japanese: *bosatsu*) 菩薩: Within Buddhism, enlightened beings who delay their own salvation to help others attain enlightenment.

deshi 弟子: Student or apprentice in traditional Japanese arts.

ganguro ガングロ (face black): A subset of the *kogyaru* who tanned their skin a deep brown, ringed their eyes with white eyeshadow, and slicked their lips white. When members of the media derided them as yamamba, they proudly owned the term, referring to themselves as "Mamba."

hakama 袴: A wide trouser-like garment worn over a kimono by men (and occasionally by women).

haniwa 埴輪: Funerary objects made of unglazed clay deposited in and around mounds of earth that covered burial sites (*kofun* in Japanese) during the Kofun and Asuka periods (c. 250–710 CE).

Izanagi 伊邪那岐: Japanese god or *kami*. His name translates loosely as "He Who Invites." His story is told in the *Kojiki* (Record of Ancient Matters, 712 CE) and the *Nihon shoki* (Chronicle of Japan, 720 CE). Along with his partner, Izanami, he is said to have created the Japanese archipelago.

Izanami 伊邪那美: Japanese god or *kami*. Her name translates loosely as "She Who Invites." She and her partner, Izanagi, created the Japanese archipelago. She died giving birth to fire. Her story is told in the *Kojiki* (Record of Ancient Matters, 712 CE) and the *Nihon shoki* (Chronicle of Japan, 720 CE).

Jizō 地蔵: One of the most beloved of the bodhisattva in Japan, considered a special guardian of children, deceased souls of children, and travelers. Statues of O-Jizō-san (the "O" is honorific), wearing a red bib, are commonly found in cemeteries and along roadsides.

jo no mai 序の舞: A dance performed by the *shite*, accompanied by flute or drums. This quiet and elegant dance (usually in five segments) is performed by dancers in the roles of beautiful women or tree spirits.

Kanze School 観世: One of the main Noh schools. Professional Noh performers belong to groups called "schools" (*ryū*), each of which traces its lineage to different teacher-performers dominant in the long history of Noh.

kappa 河童: One of the most well-known *yōkai* in Japanese media, a water imp who may be depicted as having webbed feet, green skin, beaked mouth, and a tortoise shell on its back.

kata 型: A sequence of set patterns in Noh performance and in other Japanese arts.

keisei 傾城 : Literally "castle topper," a poetic name for a high-ranking courtesan (see *oiran*) in the licensed quarters, such as the Yoshiwara of Tokyo, primarily during the seventeenth and eighteenth centuries. The *keisei* was believed to be so beautiful and beguiling she could ruin a man (or topple an empire). She was the subject of contemporary Kabuki plays, woodblock prints (*ukiyo-e*), and popular stories.

kitsune 狐: The common word for fox, and also for a shapeshifting fox *yōkai* that is the subject of numerous folktales and legends.

kofun 古墳: A tumulus, or earthen mound covering a grave, dating from the third century.

kogyaru コギャル: The term used for a group of young women from the 1990s to the late 2000s. Their street fashion, language, and behavior received massive media attention. The term "kogals" is sometimes used in English writing about them.

Kojiki (Record of Ancient Matters, 712 CE) 古事記: A compilation of origin myths of the Japanese islands, songs, and poems, the oldest extant history written in Japan. The work is written using Chinese characters in phonetic, ideographic, and logographic combinations.

kugutsume 傀儡女: Itinerant female entertainers in premodern Japan who specialized in singing and dancing and occasionally puppeteering.

Kurozuka (called *Adachigahara* in the Kanze School) 黒塚: Along with the Noh plays *Dōjōji* and *Aoi no ue,* considered one of the three female ogre plays. An elderly woman living in the mountain allows a senior monk and his retinue to stay for one night but admonishes them not to look into her room. When she goes out to gather firewood, one of the monks does look into the room. She then returns, angered, in her true form—an ogre. Although she attempts to catch the monks, their prayers save them, and she disappears into the stormy night. The first part of this play, which includes the set piece of a spinning wheel, is philosophical; the second part, terrifying but with pathos. Japanese director Kurosawa Akira used this Noh play as inspiration for the depiction of the witch in his film *Kumonosujo* (Throne of Blood, 1957).

kusemai 曲舞: A medieval dance and song, often accompanied by a fan.

Kyōgen 狂言: A traditional Japanese theatrical form stemming from the fourteenth century that stresses an earthy comedy and a gentle satirical view of all levels of society. Kyōgen plays alternated with Noh plays in a program of four or five Noh plays, but they are now often performed on their own. Kyōgen employs colloquial (to medieval times) speech, mime, and movement and vocal *kata* (patterns).

maiko 舞妓: An apprentice geisha, usually between the ages of fifteen and twenty, emblematic of Kyoto.

miko 巫女: A shrine maiden. She is responsible for performing sacred Shinto rites, such as ritual dances, and was once believed to hold a shamanic role. Some *miko* are attached to shrines; others have been itinerant.

Misora Hibari 美空ひばり: A beloved and talented singer and actress (1937–89) whose debut as a child star coincided with the early years of Japan's recovery after World War II.

Momijigari (Maple Viewing) 紅葉刈り: A Noh play written by Kanze Kojirō Nobumitsu that tells a tale of a noble woman (the *shite*) and her retinue who go to the mountains to enjoy the changing leaves. By the second act, we realize that she is the demon of Mount Togakushi. The *waki* (Taira no Koremochi) kills the demon with a divine sword given him by the bodhisattva Hachiman. This Noh play was the subject of the first film produced in Japan, in 1899.

Noh 能: Also romanized "Nō," a theatrical style that evolved in the fourteenth century that combines spoken text, dance, and music and draws heavily on classical literature and Buddhism. Noh is still a vital performing art in Japan and abroad.

oiran 花魁: A high-ranking courtesan in the licensed quarters such as the famed Yoshiwara of Tokyo, after the mid-eighteenth century. The *oiran* was frequently the subject of Kabuki dramas, woodblock prints (*ukiyo-e*), and popular stories.

oni 鬼: Demon, ogre, or monster-like being. *Oni* are often portrayed as anthropophagous with the power to alter their appearance. A type of *yōkai*.

retablo: A frame, box, or shelf enclosing decorated panels or religious objects common in South America, Mexico, and the southwestern region of the U.S.

sato 里: Village, hamlet, or flatland, a geographical location or community frequently used to indicate one's hometown or origin. In stories of the yamamba, the *sato* is in counterpoint to the mountain (*yama*).

shirabyōshi 白拍子: Female dancers in premodern Japan who performed slow, stylized dances at court dressed in costumes that resembled male attire. They were equally talented as poets, musicians, and singers. Most were itinerant.

shite 仕手: Lead actor in a Noh play. The *shite* generally wears a mask.

tayū 太夫: The highest-ranking courtesan or *oiran* in the licensed quarters, such as the famous Yoshiwara in Tokyo, until the 1750s. The *tayū* was highly educated and trained in the arts of tea, flower arranging, poetry, dance, and more and was held up as a model of womanhood in the literary works of the time. Only a few women, relatively speaking, achieved the rank of *tayū*. Of the thousands of young women who were forced into the Yoshiwara in the mid-eighteenth century, for example, only three or four ever rose to the rank of *tayū*.

Tessenkai 銕仙会: A renowned Noh performing organization led by the Kanze Tetsunojō family. Established as a branch of the Kanze School in the early eighteenth century.

tsukumogami 付喪神: Animating objects believed to acquire a soul after a hundred years of serving their owners. A type of *yōkai*.

uchiwa 団扇: Paper fans popular in summer months. A semicircle of decorated white paper is attached to a bamboo frame with a long handle. *Uchiwa* are often used to advertise events, places, and merchandise.

waki 脇: Secondary (literally, side) actor in a Noh play. Accompanies and draws out the *shite*.

Yamaguchi Momoe 山口百恵: Hugely popular singer (b. 1959) and movie star who retired from show business at age twenty-one.

yamamba gashira 山婆がしら: A long wig, generally brown or white, worn only in Act II of *Yamamba*.

yōkai 妖怪: A class of strange and supernatural beings or creatures in Japanese folklore that includes *oni* (demon, ogre, and monster) and *tsukumogami* (animating object).

Zeami Motokiyo 世阿弥元清: Noh actor and playwright (c. 1363–c. 1443). He wrote over fifty Noh plays along with significant treatises on the art and poetics of the Noh theater.

Endnotes

LOCATING THE YAMAMBA

1 Translations of these stories are available in Fanny Hagin Mayer, ed., *The Yanagita Kunio Guide to Japanese Folk Tales* (Bloomington: University of Indiana Press, 1986): 44–46, 110–14.

2 Yoshida Atsuhiko, *Mukashibanashi no kōkogaku: Yamauba to Jōmon no megami* (Tokyo: Chūō Kōronsha, 1992): 31–34.

3 Komatsu, "Kaisetsu: *Tengu to yamauba*," in *Kaii no minzokugaku*, vol. 5, ed. Komatsu Kazuhiko (Tokyo: Kawade Shobō, 2000): 428.

4 William Wayne Farris, *Japan's Medieval Population: Famine, Fertility, and Warfare in a Transformative Age* (Honolulu: University of Hawai'i Press, 2006): 128.

5 Farris: 149.

6 Mizuta Noriko, "Yamauba no yume: Joron to shite," in *Yamauba tachi no monogatari: Josei no genkei to katarinaoshi*, ed. Mizuta Noriko and Kitada Sachie (Tokyo: Gakugei Shorin, 2002): 13.

7 Miyake Hitoshi, *Shugendō: Essays on the Structure of Japanese Folk Religion* (Ann Arbor: Center for Japanese Studies, University of Michigan, 2001): 78–79.

8 Baba Akiko, *Oni no kenkyū* (Tokyo: Chikuma Shobō, 1988; first published 1971): 279.

9 Sugawara no Takasue no musume, *As I Crossed a Bridge of Dreams: Recollections of a Woman in Eleventh-Century Japan*, trans. Ivan Morris (New York: Dial, 1971): 47.

10 Baba, *Oni no kenkyū*: 276–77.

11 Yanagita Kunio, *Teihon Yanagita Kunioshū*, vol. 4 (Tokyo: Chikuma Shobō, 1968): 378–80.

12 Claire R. Farrer, *Women and Folklore* (Austin: University of Texas Press, 1975): xiii.

13 Mizuta, "Yamauba no yume": 10–12.

14 Mizuta: 12–15.
15 Mizuta: 10.
16 Yanagita, *Teihon Yanagita Kunioshū*: 285–437.
17 Yoshida, *Mukashibanashi no kōkogaku*: 31–34.
18 Komatsu, "Kaisetsu": 429–30.
19 Komatsu Kazuhiko, *Hyōrei shinkō ron* (Tokyo: Kōdansha, 1994): 283.
20 Komatsu, "Kaisetsu": 432.

A YAMAMBA SHRINEBOX

1 The print is named "Yamauba Combing Her Hair and Kintoki," dated around 1801. In the Metropolitan Museum of Art collection, New York. Online at https://www.metmuseum.org/art/collection/search/54858.
2 Monica Bethe and Karen Brazell, trans., "Yamamba, Attributed to Zeami," in *Traditional Japanese Theater: An Anthology of Plays*, ed. Karen Brazell (New York: Columbia University Press, 1998): 207–25.
3 Monica Bethe and Karen Brazell, "Introduction to Yamanba," The Japanese Performing Arts Resource Center (undated). Online at http://www.glopad.org/jparc/?q=en/node/22775.
4 Nagumo Seiichi, Kubota Mitsuru, and Shigeyama Yoshinori, directors, *Osen*, 2008. This ten-episode TV series aired on Nippon Television Network Corporation, Tokyo.
5 Michael Bathgate, *The Fox's Craft in Japanese Religion and Folklore: Shapeshifters, Transformations, and Duplicities* (New York: Routledge, 2003).
6 Yanagita Kunio and Sasaki Kizen, *Folk Legends from Tono: Japan's Spirits, Deities, and Phantastic Creatures*, trans. Ronald A. Morse (Lantham, MD: Rowman and Littlefield, 2015).
7 Iva Lakić Parać, "Bodhisattva Jizo and Folk Religious Influences: Elements of Folk Religion in Jizo's Understanding in Japan," *Asian Studies* 4 (1), 2016: 115–29.
8 Miki Fumio, *Haniwa*, trans. Gina Lee Barnes (New York: Weatherhill, 1974).
9 Laura Miller, "Those Naughty Teenage Girls: Japanese *Kogals*, Slang, and Media Assessments," *Journal of Linguistic Anthropology* 14, no. 2 (2004): 225–47.

Recommended Readings

Aoyama, Tomoko. "Mad Old Japanese Woman Writes Back from an Attic of her Own." *AUMLA* (2012): 15–34.

Baba Akiko. *Oni no kenkyū*. Tokyo: Chikuma Shobō, 1988; first published 1971.

Bethe, Monica, and Karen Brazell. *Nō as Performance: An Analysis of the Kuse Scene of Yamanba*. Cornell East Asia Papers. Ithaca: Cornell University, 1978.

_____. "Yamamba." In *Traditional Japanese Theater: An Anthology of Plays*, edited by Karen Brazell. New York: Columbia University Press, 1998: 207–25.

Bullock, Julia C. "Burning Down the House: Fantasies of Liberation in the Era of 'Women's Lib.'" *Japanese Language and Literature* 49.2 (October 2015): 233–57.

Copeland, Rebecca. "Art Beyond Language: Japanese Women Artists and the Feminist Imagination." In *Imagination without Borders: Feminist Artist Tomiyama Taeko and Social Responsibility*, edited by Laura Hein and Rebecca Jennison. Ann Arbor: Center for Japanese Studies, University of Michigan, 2010: 51–67.

_____. "Kirino Natsuo Meets Izanami: Angry Divas Talking Back." In *Diva Nation: Female Icons from Japanese Cultural History*, edited by Laura Miller and Rebecca Copeland. Berkeley: University of California Press, 2018: 13–33.

_____. "Mythical Bad Girls: The Corpse, the Crone, and the Snake."

In *Bad Girls of Japan*, edited by Laura Miller and Jan Bardsley. New York: Palgrave Macmillan, 2005: 15–32.

Ehrlich, Linda. "Kannon-sama and the Spirit of Compassion in Japanese Cinema." In *Goddesses: Dialectics of the Feminine in Japanese Audiovisual Culture*, edited by Lorenzo Torres. Lexington, KY: Lexington Press, 2018: 1–16.

_____. *Yamamba's Mountains*. Poetry, with illustrations by Yūko Kimura and Maria Alilovic. Designed by Horse and Buggy Press (Durham, NC), 2018.

Foster, Michael Dylan. *The Book of Yōkai: Mysterious Creatures of Japanese Folklore*. Berkeley: University of California Press, 2015.

Hansen, Kelly. "Deviance and Decay in the Body of a Modern Mountain Witch: Ōba Minako's '*Yamanba no bishō*.'" *Japanese Language and Literature* 48. 1. Introduction to the Special Section: "In Her Voice: Interrogating Gendered Notions of Gaze and Body" (April 2014): 151–72.

Holloway, David. "Topographies of Intimacy: Sex and Shibuya in Hasegawa Junko's *Prisoner of Solitude*." *US-Japan Women's Journal* 49 (2016): 51–67.

_____. "The Unmaking of a Diva: Kanehara Hitomi's Comfortable Anonymity." In *Diva Nation: Female Icons from Japanese Cultural History*, edited by Laura Miller and Rebecca Copeland. Berkeley: University of California Press, 2018: 168–84.

Hulvey, S. Yumiko. "Myths and Monsters: The Female Body as the Site for Political Agendas." In *Body Politics and the Fictional Double*, edited by Debra Walker King. Bloomington: Indiana University Press, 2000: 71–88.

Hurley, Adrienne. "Demons, Transnational Subjects, and the Fiction of Ōba Minako." In *Oe and Beyond: Fiction in Contemporary Japan*, edited by Stephen Snyder and Philip Gabriel. Honolulu: University of Hawai'i Press, 1999: 89–103.

Japanese Performing Arts Resource Center (JPARC). http://www.glopad.org/jparc/.

Kanai Mieko. "Yamamba" (1973). In *Kanai Mieko zentanpen*. Vol. 1. Tokyo: Nihon Bungeisha, 1992: 557–79.

Kawai Hayao. "The Woman Who Eats Nothing." In *The Japanese Psyche: Major Motifs in the Fairy Tales of Japan,* translated by Kawai Hayao and Sachiko Reece. Dallas: Spring Publications, 1988: 27–45.

Komatsu Kazuhiko. "Kaisetsu: *Tengu to yamauba*." In *Kaii no minzokugaku,* vol. 5, edited by Komatsu Kazuhiko. Tokyo: Kawade Shobō, 2000: 417–34.

Li, Michelle Osterfeld. *Ambiguous Bodies: Reading the Grotesque in Japanese Setsuwa Tales*. Stanford: Stanford University Press, 2009.

Mayer, Fanny Hagin, ed. and trans. *The Yanagita Kunio Guide to Japanese Folk Tales*. Bloomington: University of Indiana Press, 1986.

Miller, Laura. "Girl Culture in East Asia." *Transnational Asia: An Online Interdisciplinary Journal* 1.2 (2017).

_____. "Searching for Charisma Queen Himiko." In *Diva Nation: Female Icons from Japanese Cultural History,* edited by Laura Miller and Rebecca Copeland. Berkeley: University of California Press, 2018: 51–76.

_____. "Those Naughty Teenage Girls: Japanese *Kogals*, Slang, and Media Assessments." *Journal of Linguistic Anthropology* 14.2 (2004): 225–47.

Mizuta Noriko. "Madonna as Self-Begetting Mountain Witch: Ōba Minako's Mythmaking." *The Force of Vision: Proceedings of the XIIIth Congress of the International Comparative Literature Association* 6 (1995): 441–47.

Mizuta Noriko and Kitada Sachie, eds. *Yamamba-tachi no monogatari: Josei no genkei to katarinaoshi*. Tokyo: Gakugei Shorin, 2002.

Ōba Minako. "Candle Fish." Translated by Yukiko Tanaka. In *Unmapped Territories: New Women's Fiction from Japan,* edited by Yukiko Tanaka. Seattle: Women in Translation, 1991: 18–38.

_____. "The Smile of a Mountain Witch." Translated by Noriko Mizuta Lippit. In *Japanese Women Writers: Twentieth Century Short Fiction,* edited by Noriko Mizuta Lippit and Kyoko Iriye Selden. New York: M. E. Sharpe, 1991: 194–206.

Ōba Minako and Mizuta Noriko. *Taidan: Yamanba no iru fūkei*. Tokyo: Tahata Shoten, 1995.

Quinn, Shelley Fenno. *Developing Zeami: The Noh Actor's Attunement in Practice*. Honolulu: University of Hawai'i Press, 2005.

Reider, Noriko. *Japanese Demon Lore: Oni from Ancient Times to the Present*. Logan, UT: Utah State University Press, 2010.

_____. *Mountain Witches: Yamauba*. Logan, UT: Utah State University Press, 2021.

_____. "Transformation of the Oni: From the Frightening and Diabolical to the Cute and Sexy," *Asian Folklore Studies* 62.1 (2003): 133–57.

_____. "Yamauba: Representation of the Japanese Mountain Witch in the Muromachi and Edo Periods." *International Journal of Asian Studies* 2.2 (2005): 239–64.

_____. "Yamauba versus Oni-Women: Devouring and Helping Yamauba Are Two Sides of One Coin." *Asian Ethnology* 78. 2 (2019).

Sherif, Ann. "Art as Activism: Tomiyama Taeko and the Marukis." In *Imagination without Borders: Feminist Artist Tomiyama Taeko and Social Responsibility*, edited by Laura Hein and Rebecca Jennison. Ann Arbor: University of Michigan Center for Japanese Studies, 2010: 29–50.

Shirane, Haruo. *Japan and the Culture of the Four Seasons: Nature, Literature, and the Arts*. New York: Columbia University Press, 2012.

Smethurst, Mae. *The Artistry of Aeschylus and Zeami: A Comparative Study of Greek Tragedy and Nō*. Princeton: Princeton University Press, 1989.

_____. *Dramatic Representations of Filial Piety: Five Noh in Translation, with an Introduction*. Ithaca, NY: East Asia Program, Cornell University, 1998.

Tawada Yoko. "The Man With Two Mouths." Translated by Margaret Mitsutani. *Marvels & Tales*, vol. 27, no. 2, *The Fairy Tale in Japan* (2013): 321–29.

Tsushima Yūko. *Woman Running in the Mountains*. Translated by Geraldine Harcourt. 1st American edition (New York: Pantheon, 1991).

Ury, Marian, trans. and ed. *Tales of Times Now Past: Sixty-Two Stories from a Medieval Japanese Collection*. Berkeley: University of California Press, 1979.

Viswanathan, Meera "In Pursuit of Yamamba: The Question of Female Resistance." In *The Woman's Hand: Gender and Theory in Japanese Women's Writing*, edited by Paul Gordon Schalow and Janet A. Walker. Stanford: Stanford University Press, 1996: 242–43.

Wilson, Michiko N. "Ōba Minako the Raconteur: Refashioning a *Yamauba* Tale." *Marvels & Tales*, vol. 27., no. 2, *The Fairy Tale in Japan* (2013): 218–33.

Yoshida Atsuhiko. *Mukashibanashi no kōkogaku: Yamauba to Jōmon no megami*. Tokyo: Chūō Kōronsha, 1992.

Zeami. *Yamamba*. Translated by Monica Bethe and Karen Brazell. In *Traditional Japanese Theater: An Anthology of Plays*, edited by Karen Brazell. New York: Columbia University Press, 1998: 207–25.

Contributors

MARIA ALILOVIC was born in Louisville, Kentucky, after her parents immigrated to the United States following the Bosnian Civil War in 1996. Her family settled in Bedford, Ohio, where she graduated from Bedford High School as valedictorian. She received her Bachelor of Science in Art Education with licensure to teach grades pre-K–12 in Visual Arts and a Bachelor of Arts in English with licensure to teach grades 7–12 in Integrated Language Arts from Case Western Reserve University in Cleveland, Ohio, in 2017. She also received her Master of Arts in Art Education from Case Western Reserve University and has been teaching high school art in the Cleveland Metropolitan School District since 2018. Alilovic is an artist and a writer, seeking to communicate her family's experience during and after the war in her artwork. Her artwork focuses on themes of memory, history, transition, and appropriation.

REBECCA COPELAND is Professor of Japanese literature at Washington University in St. Louis. Her publications include *Lost Leaves: Women Writers of Meiji Japan* (University of Hawai'i Press, 2000), *The Modern Murasaki: Writing by Women of Meiji Japan* (with Melek Ortabasi, Columbia University Press, 2006), *Woman Critiqued: Translated Essays on Japanese Women's Writing* (University of Hawai'i Press, 2006), and *The Father-Daughter Plot: Japanese Literary Women and the Law of the Father* (with Esperanza Ramirez-Christensen, University of Hawai'i Press, 2001). She has translated works of Uno Chiyo, Hirabayashi Taiko, and Kirino Natsuo. Her translation of Kirino's *The Goddess Chronicle* (Grove Press, 2014) received the 2014–15 Japan-U.S. Friendship Commission Prize for the Translation of Japanese Literature. "Blue Ridge Yamamba," along with her debut novel, *The Kimono Tattoo* (Brother Mockingbird Publishing, 2021), mark her shift to writing fiction.

LINDA C. EHRLICH is an independent scholar who has published extensively about world cinema and about traditional theatre in *Film Quarterly, Cinema Journal, Senses of Cinema, Film Criticism, Ethnomusicology, Cinema Scope, Framework,* and *Journal of Religion and Film,* among others. Her book *Cinematic Reveries* (Peter Lang Publishers, 2013) explores the intersection of prose poetry and cinema. *Cinematic Landscapes,* her first book (co-edited with David Desser), is an anthology of essays on the interface between the visual arts and cinemas of China and Japan (University of Texas Press, 1994; reprinted in 2008). Her second edited book, *The Cinema of Víctor Erice: An Open Window,* appeared in the Scarecrow Press Filmmakers' Series (#72) in 2000 (with an expanded paperback edition in 2007). Ehrlich's taped commentary on *The Spirit of the Beehive (El espíritu de la colmena,* dir. Víctor Erice, 1973) appears on the Criterion DVD of that film. Her full-length commentary is a key feature of the Milestone Film and Video 25th-anniversary DVD/Blu-ray of *Maborosi* (dir. Kore-eda Hirokazu). In addition, she has published poetry in *International Poetry Review, The Bitter Oleander, Southern Poetry Review, Literary Arts Hawaii, Pinesong,* and other literary journals. Ehrlich's book on Japanese director Kore-eda Hirokazu was published by Palgrave Macmillan in 2020. Dr. Ehrlich has taught at Duke University, Case Western Reserve University, and the University of Tennessee/Knoxville and on two Semester-at-Sea voyages.

DAVID HOLLOWAY is Assistant Professor of Japanese Literature at the University of Rochester, where he teaches courses on literature, culture, and society. He has published in a variety of journals including *US-Japan Women's Journal* and *Japanese Language and Literature.* His current book project, *The End of Transgression: Gender, Body, Nation,* explores issues of deviance, body, and literature in contemporary fiction by Japanese women. In addition, David is working on a second book project that brings to the fore Japanese discourse in print and visual media about HIV and AIDS. His other scholarly interests include Japan's "lost decade," sex and sexuality, youth culture, and visual and media studies.

LAURA MILLER is the Ei'ichi Shibusawa-Seigo Arai Endowed Professor of Japanese Studies and Professor of History at the University of Missouri-St. Louis. She received her PhD in linguistic anthropology from the

University of California–Los Angeles in 1988. Miller has published widely on Japan, including more than eighty articles and book chapters on Japanese culture and language. The topics have included English loanwords in Japanese, young women's slang and *gyaru moji* (girl's characters), *purikura* self-photography, the Japanese divination industry and tarot cards, Elevator Girls, and figures from history such as Himiko, a third-century shaman ruler, and Abe no Seimei, a Heian-period wizard. She is the author of *Beauty Up: Exploring Contemporary Japanese Body Aesthetics* (University of California Press, 2006), and co-editor of four other books, including *Diva Nation: Female Icons from Japanese Cultural History* (with Copeland, University of California Press, 2018), *Modern Girls on the Go: Gender, Mobility, and Labor in Japan* (with Freedman and Yano, Stanford University Press, 2013), *Manners and Mischief: Gender, Power, and Etiquette in Japan* (with Bardsley, University of California Press, 2011), and *Bad Girls of Japan* (with Bardsley, Palgrave Macmillan, 2005). She is currently doing research on the occult and divination industry in Japan and on Japanese gendered linguistic ideology. Miller serves as Associate Editor for a project in progress, *The International Encyclopedia of Linguistic Anthropology*, to be published by Wiley Blackwell.

MIZUTA NORIKO is a poet, translator, comparative literature scholar, former professor at the University of Southern California, former president of Jōsai International University and chancellor of Jōsai Educational Corporation, and current chancellor and director of the International Institute for Media and Women's Studies. Along with Kyoko Selden, Dr. Mizuta was a pioneer in the translation of works by modern Japanese women writers, as represented by the anthology *Japanese Women Writers: Twentieth Century Short Fiction* (M. E. Sharpe, 1991). She also pioneered the field of feminist literary criticism in Japan, as represented by her 1981 study *Hiroin kara hiiroo e: Josei no jiga to hyōgen* (From Heroine to Hero: Female Self and Expression), and she was among the first to explore the metaphorical power of the yamamba; see particularly her 1994 published interview on the topic with the author Ōba Minako, *Taidan: Yamamba no iru fūkei* (Dialogue: The Yamamba Environment). An accomplished poet, Dr. Mizuta was awarded the Cikada Prize in Poetry in honor of Nobel Laureate Harry Martinson in 2013. Among her poetry collections translated into

English are *The Road Home* (translated by Jordan Smith, Josai University Press, 2015). In 2011 she was awarded the Pro Cultura Hungarica prize and in 2013 the Commander's Cross of the Order of Merit of Hungary (civil division).

OHMORI KAYO is a music therapist and reciter of poetry who lives in Chiba, Japan, outside Tokyo. Originally from Sakaide-shi on the island of Shikoku, she met Linda Ehrlich when Ehrlich was an American Field Service exchange student in high school. Ohmori was inspired by Ehrlich and came to be interested in poems when Ehrlich brought her a poetry book. In addition to the Japanese translation of "Yamamba's Mountains," Ohmori drew the calligraphy of the word "yamamba."

NORIKO TSUNODA REIDER is a Professor of Japanese at Miami University of Ohio. Her PhD is in Japanese literature. Her research and publications are primarily in Japanese literature and folklore. She has published *Seven Demon Stories from Medieval Japan* (Utah State University Press, 2016), *Japanese Demon Lore: Oni, from Ancient Times to the Present* (Utah State University Press, 2010), *Tales of the Supernatural in Early Modern Japan* (Edwin Mellen Press, 2002), and many articles including "*Spirited Away*: Film of the Fantastic and Evolving Japanese Folk Symbols" in *Film Criticism* (2005). In her most recent work, *Mountain Witches: Yamauba* (Utah State University Press, 2021), she focuses on the yamamba. She is a certified Japanese tea instructor.

ANN SHERIF earned a PhD in Japanese Literature at the University of Michigan and is a Professor of East Asian Studies at Oberlin College. Her books include *Japan's Cold War: Media, Literature, and the Law* (Columbia University Press, 2009) and *Mirror: The Essays and Fiction of Kōda Aya* (University of Hawai'i Press, 1999). She has published widely on Japanese literature, literary criticism, book history in East Asia, and nuclear weapons and the environment. Her research has been supported by fellowships from NEH, Fulbright, and the Japan Foundation. Sherif was fortunate to have the Uzawas, a professional Noh family, as her host family when she was studying abroad in Japan. Since her student days, Sherif has regularly attended Noh performances and introduces students to Noh and other Japanese performing arts in her classes.

MARIANNE TARCOV is an Assistant Professor of Japanese Studies at McGill University in Montreal, Canada. She is at work on the book project *Screening Open Secrets of War, Mass Culture, and Hometown in Twentieth-Century Japanese Poetry*. She has published two articles in *Journal of Japanese Language and Literature* and has guest edited a special section of the journal titled *Bodies in Pain, Flux, and Pleasure: Transgressive Femininity in Japanese Media and Literature.* Her translations of modern Japanese poetry have appeared in *Asymptote*, *Poetry Kanto*, *Octopus*, and elsewhere, and her translations have been nominated for the Pushcart Prize.

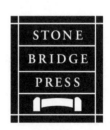

Stone Bridge Press books are available at booksellers worldwide and online.
sbp@stonebridge.com • www.stonebridge.com